청소년 영어성경공부 교재 Vol. 1

We Want to Be Real Christians!

kmc

이현주

감리교신학대학교 영어담당 교수

이화여자대학교 영문학과를 졸업하고 동대학원에서 영문학 석 · 박사학위와 Wesley Theological Seminary에서 목회학 박사 학위를 받았다. 사립학교 영어교사 자격증을 소유하고 있으며, 미국 Teachers College Columbia University에서 TESOL Certificate도 취득했다.

저서로는 『자, 이제 제대로 된 영어를 하자』, 『영작문 한 권으로 따라잡기』, 『난생 처음 쓰는 영어일기: 초급편』, 『난생 처음 쓰는 영어일기: 직장인편』, 『논리가 살아나는 영어 에세이 쓰기』, 『1% 더 실천하는 엄마가 영어 영재 만든다』, 『영어로 신학 맛보기』, 『초기 개신교 선교사의 시와 헌신: 그 부르심의 길』 등이 있으며, 『아서 왕의 죽음 1, 2』, 『이화』를 비롯한 많은 역서가 있다.

We Want to Be Real Christians!

펴낸날 | 2013년 12월 24일

펴낸이 | 전용재

엮은곳 | 기독교대한감리회 교육국
　　　　www.kmcedu.or.kr

엮은이 | 정현범

지은이 | 이현주

그린이 | 최정을

디자인 | 조영라

펴낸곳 | 기독교대한감리회 출판국 · 도서출판 kmc
　　　　손인선
　　　　서울시 종로구 세종대로 149 감리회관 16층
　　　　TEL. 02-399-2008　FAX. 02-399-2085
　　　　www.kmcmall.co.kr
　　　　methpub@chol.com

등　록 | 제2-1607호 (1993. 9. 4)

인　쇄 | 신일문화사

ISBN　978-89-8430-627-1 04230
　　　　978-89-8430-626-4 04230 (세트)

값　7,000원

▶ 이 도서의 국립중앙도서관 출판시도서목록(CIP)은 서지정보유통지원시스템 홈페이지(http://seoji.nl.go.kr)와
　　국가자료공동목록시스템(http://www.nl.go.kr/kolisnet)에서 이용하실 수 있습니다. (CIP제어번호: CIP2013025627)

My heart rejoices in the LORD;

…

There is no one holy like the LORD;

there is no one besides you;

there is no Rock like our God.

(1 Samuel 2:1-2)

이 책은 하나님 말씀을 영어로 배우는 책입니다!

감리교신학대학교의 영어 교수로 재직하면서 제가 꼭 해보고 싶었고 또 소명이라 믿었던 일은 영어성경학교 교재 개발이었습니다. 『자, 이제 제대로 된 영어를 하자』(평민사), 『영작문 한 권으로 따라잡기』(다락원), 『난생 처음 쓰는 영어일기』 초급편, 직장인편(넥서스), 『논리가 살아나는 영어 에세이 쓰기』(넥서스), 『영어로 신학 맛보기』(신앙과 지성사) 등 영어 교재를 계속 집필하면서 영어성경학교 교재를 함께 개발하려 하였지만 원하는 결과를 얻지 못하였습니다. 여러 번 시도하였지만 계속 이뤄지지 않는 상황을 접하면서 영어성경학교 교재 개발은 저의 소명이 아니라 생각하고 포기했습니다. 그러나 이와 같은 저의 생각은 Wesley Theological Seminary에서 목회학 박사 과정을 공부하면서 변화하기 시작했습니다.

제 목회학 박사 논문 제목은 *An Intensive English Bible School Program for Under Privileged Children at Sae-Onyang Church*입니다. 논문 준비를 위해 실제 교회 현장에서 영어 프로그램을 운영해보며 현장의 소리를 듣게 되었습니다. 미자립 교회나 지방의 교회에서 영어로 된 프로그램에 대한 요구의 소리를 들었습니다. 또 경제적, 사회적 환경 때문에 영어 교육을 따로 받지 못하는 아이들의 모습도 보았습니다. 영어성경학교 교재를 개발하는 것이 이들 교회와 아이들에게 조금이나마 도움이 되지 않을까 하는 생각이 다시 들었습니다.

목회학 박사 과정은 제게 영어성경교재 개발의 방법론을 일깨워 주었습니다. 제가 집필한 일련의 영어 관련 서적들은 대부분 어떻게 하면 영어 능력을 증진시키는가에 목적 및 중점을 두었습니다. 그러나 공부하는 과정에서 저는 영어성경학교 교재 개발의 주목적은 하나님 말씀을 바르게 전달하는 것이라는 사실을 깨달았습니다. '영어는 단지 하나님의 말씀을 가르치는 도구'라는 분명한 생각을 가지게 된 것이죠.

이 책의 목적은 구약의 인물들을 중심으로 하나님의 말씀을 배우는 것입니다!

이를 배우는 과정에 영어 교육적 방법론을 도입하였습니다. 각 장마다 영어의 네 가지 능력, 듣기(listening), 말하기(speaking), 읽기(reading), 쓰기(writing) 능력을 종합적으로 증진시킬 수 있는 코너를 구성하였습니다.

〈Who Am I?〉 코너는 영어를 들으며 누구에 대해 말하는지 알아보는 장으로, 주로 듣기와 읽기 훈련을 하는 부분입니다. 이 부분에서는 책의 마지막 부분에 마련해둔 영영사전(Index Dictionary)을 활용하여 영어 어휘 공부를 함께 할 수 있도록 하였습니다.

〈Grammar Points〉 코너는 중학교 교과서에서 나오는 기본 문법들을 알기 쉽게 공부하는 부분입니다. 초등학교 5, 6학년 학생의 경우 중학교에서 배울 문법을 미리 배워본다는 점에서, 중학생의 경우 학교에서 배우는 문법을 점검한다는 점에서 권하고 싶은 부분입니다.

〈Let's Talk〉 코너는 말하기 훈련을 하는 부분입니다. 앞의 본문에서 나온 문장을 패턴 중심으로 엄선해 살아 있는 실생활 표현을 익히는 것을 목적으로 하였습니다.

〈Confession & Prayer〉 코너는 읽기와 쓰기를 훈련할 수 있는 부분입니다. 이 코너는 특히 하나님의 말씀을 다시 한 번 진중하게 생각해보고 서로의 생각을 나눠보는 부분이기도 합니다. 영어로 기도를 쓰는 훈련을 할 수 있는 코너도 마련해 두었습니다. 영어권 어린아이들이 쓴 기도문이나 전통적인 좋은 기도문을 소개한 후 이 기도문에 따라 영어로 직접 자신만의 기도문을 써보고 말해보는 훈련도 할 수 있도록 했습니다.

〈A Poem & Song〉은 노래를 통해 하나님의 말씀을 기억하고 영어 능력을 증진시키는 부분입니다. www.sheilahamil.co.uk에 들어가 직접 애니메이션을 보면서 노래를 함께 익힐 수 있다는 점에서 매우 효과적입니다.

이 책의 가장 큰 특징은 교사가 꼭
원어민이어야 할 필요는 없다는 점입니다!

전문 영어 성우가 읽는 오디오와 www.sheilahamil.co.uk에서 보여주는 동영상을 활용하면 원어민이 아니더라도 충분히 이 책을 가르칠 수 있습니다. 또 감리교신학대학교의 평생교육원에서 이 책을 활용하는 방법을 공부하는 교사 프로그램을 운영하고 있습니다. 제가 직접 운영하는 이 프로그램에서는 이 책을 어떻게 활용하는지에 대한 방법을 같이 연구하며 필요한 활동(activities) 자료들을 공유합니다.

이 책은 영어성경 교재를 개발하고자 하는 제 바람의 첫발입니다. 이 첫발을 내딛도록 도와주신 하나님께 깊은 감사를 드립니다. 쉽지 않은 여건에서도 저를 믿어주시고 도와주신 평생교육원장 장성배 교수님과 감리회 본부 교육국의 정현범 목사님께 감사드립니다. 힘든 상황을 겪을 때 제게 영적으로 힘을 주신 서초중앙교회 조세제 목사님께 감사드립니다. 그리고 무엇보다도 편집진들에게 감사드립니다. 이들은 모두 국내 유수 영어 전문 출판사의 편집을 하는 이들로 봉사하는 마음으로 이 책을 함께 작업하였습니다. 마지막으로 항상 일에 바쁜 아내와 엄마를 이해하고 사랑으로 기다려주는 가족들에게 감사와 사랑을 보냅니다.

이현주

국제화 시대의 신앙인이라면
자신의 신앙을 교류할 수 있는 힘을 길러야…

오늘을 사는 현대인들, 특별히 경쟁 구조 속에 있는 현대인들에게 가장 큰 키워드 가운데 하나가 국제화입니다. 한국의 대외적인 국가 경쟁력의 가장 기본에는 국제화에 대한 이해가 매우 절실히 요구됩니다. 국제화는 매우 포괄적인 의미를 가지고 있지만, 전 세계가 상호 교통하며 공통의 관심사를 교류하는 것을 의미합니다. 이러한 교류의 기본적이고 필수적인 수단이 바로 영어입니다. 혹자들은 영어를 미국언어로 생각하는 사람들이 있습니다. 이는 시대착오적인 생각입니다. 이제 더 이상 영어는 한 나라에 귀속된 국가언어가 아닌 국제어임을 알아야 합니다.

세계적으로 유명한 국내의 한 기업은 이미 그 입사전형에 외국어 능력 여부를 중요한 잣대로 활용하고 있습니다. 하지만, 이 기업의 외국어 항목에 영어는 이미 사라진 지 오래입니다. 영어는 이미 국제어로 인식되어 기본적으로 누구나 해야 하는 필수적인 언어라는 인식이 있기 때문입니다. 영어는 오늘을 사는 현대 한국인들에게 선택의 영역이 아닌, 필수의 영역으로 자리잡고 있으며, 이러한 인식은 세대를 내려갈수록 더 커지고 있음을 잘 알 수 있습니다.

영어 조기교육 열풍은 어제 오늘의 일이 아닙니다. 아무리 경제적으로 어렵다 하여도 가계의 지출에서 자녀 교육비(특별히 지나칠 정도로 과한 영어 사교육은 문제로 인식되지만)는 어김없이 할당되어 있어 그 누구도 이 경쟁에서 뒤처지지 않기 위해 영어 학습에 매진하는 모습을 보여줍니다. 필수적으로 영어 학습을 할 수밖에 없는 이러한 시대적 상황에서 우리 아이들은 국제 사회의 일원으로 자신의 신앙을 교류할 수 있는 힘을 키울 필요가 있습니다. 그래서 감리교신학대학교에서 영어 교수로 섬기고 있는 이현주 박사의 『We Want to Be Real Christians!』가 출간된 것이 무척이나 반갑습니다. 바로 영어와 함께 신앙의 기초를 쌓을 수 있는 훌륭한 교재이기 때문이죠.

저자인 이현주 박사는 영어와 신학으로 박사학위를 가지고 있는 훌륭한 학자이자 교사입니다. 오랜 시간 대학에서 가르친 노하우와 지식을 봉헌해, 영어를 통해서 신앙의 기초를 더욱 단단히 다질 수 있는 훌륭한 책을 한국 교회에 선물로 내놓았습니다. 구약의 인물들을 중심으로 구성된 이 책을 통해서 독자들은 신앙의 삶을 살았던 이들의 이야기를 영어로 경험하게 될 것입니다. 이 책은 어린 초등학생부터 영어의 기초를 다시 점검하고자 하는 모든 신앙인들이 사용할 수 있도록 쉽고, 재미있게 구성된 책입니다.

교회도 국제화의 흐름을 피해갈 수 없습니다. 영어를 통한 신앙 교육과 훈련, 또한 말씀을 통한 영어 체득, 이 두 마리의 토끼를 감리교신학대학교 이현주 교수의 『We Want to Be Real Christians!』를 통해 경험하시길 추천합니다. 특별히 교회에서 이 책을 통해 교회학교 교육의 교재로 활용한다면 이야기 중심의 구약에 대한 이해도를 확연히 높일 수 있는 기회를 갖게 될 것입니다.

감리교신학대학교 총장 박종천

글로벌 크리스천을 양성해야 하는 우리들

영어공부 교재의 베스트셀러 작가인 이현주 교수님의 『We Want to Be Real Christians!』가 출간된 것을 기쁘게 생각하고 축하드립니다. 일반 영어공부 교재 분야에서의 명성은 이미 들으셨을 줄 믿습니다. 이제 그가 그동안의 영어교재 집필의 노하우와 감리교신학대학교에서 쌓았던 영어 교수로서의 경험, 그리고 Wesley Theological Seminary의 D. Min. 학위를 취득하면서 축적한 신학적 기반을 바탕으로 영어성경공부 교재를 출간하였습니다. 미래 교회와 지구촌 사회를 책임질 글로벌 크리스천을 양성해야 하는 교회학교 교육 담당자들에게는 엄청난 희소식이 될 줄 믿습니다. 이 영어성경공부 교재의 발간은 감리교회의 교회학교 교육이 세계를 향해 진일보할 수 있는 중요한 계기가 될 것입니다.

특히 이현주 교수님은 감리교신학대학교 평생교육원의 영어목회훈련센터에서 "영어성경공부 지도자 양성반"을 운영하고 있고, 이 책은 그 훈련 과정의 주요 교재가 될 것입니다. 이 교재와 훈련 과정을 통해서 감리교회의 교회학교가 글로벌 크리스천을 양성하는 데 도움이 되기를 기도합니다.

감리교신학대학교 선교학 교수, 평생교육원장 장성배

진정한 크리스천의 길로 나아가는 데 필요한 나침반

시대의 흐름에 발맞춰 교회 안에서도 전도나 교회 부흥을 위한 일종의 수단으로 영어 프로그램을 도입하기 시작한 지는 꽤 되었지만, 실제적인 성과는 거두지 못하고 있는 실정입니다. 이에 교육국에서는 진정한 감리교인으로 다음 세대를 이끌어갈 수 있는 영성과 지성을 겸비한 글로벌 리더를 양성하기 위해, 심혈을 기울여 '인물별 영어성경공부 교재'를 개발하였습니다. 오랜 시간과 고민, 그리고 기도를 통해 개발한 이 교재 속에는 진정한 크리스천의 심성과 자세의 모범을 보여주는 성경 속 인물들이 등장합니다. 이 인물들과 하나님의 관계를 영어로 이해하고 하나님의 말씀을 다시 한 번 생각하며 진정한 크리스천의 길로 나아가는 데 필요한 나침반이 될 수 있으리라 믿습니다. 이 책은 교육국과 감신대 영어목회훈련센터가 협력하여 개발하였으며, 감신대 평생교육원에서는 이 교재를 활용할 수 있도록 지도자 훈련 과정을 강의로 개설하였습니다. 이 책을 집필한 저자인 이현주 교수가 직접 지도자 훈련 과정을 강의합니다. 이를 통해 양성된 지도자들은 우리 아이들의 주일 공과공부 및 주 5일제에 따른 주말 프로그램 등의 교재로 이 책을 알차게 활용할 수 있을 것입니다.

교육국 총무직무대리 정현범

Study God's Precious Word! God's Word Is A Living Word!

Greetings to you all, dear children, as you study God's precious word. May I recommend this project of Professor Hyunju Lee to you.

Always remember God's word is a living word, which will speak to your heart the more you read it.

In Isaiah 55:11 we learn that the word that goes out from God's mouth, will never return to him empty without accomplishing all that he desires and will achieve the purpose for which it was sent.

It is a word we must revere, respect, and try to memorise so we can draw from it like water from a deep well. Drink from it and drench yourself in it. If a particular verse calls out to you, stay with it, bathe in it before you continue reading.

May God's word open your eyes and fill your hearts with His wisdom, His love and peace.

My love and blessings to you all *Sheila*

* Reverend Sheila Hamil has been working on the project called KALEIDOSCOPE OF CHARACTERS, a collection of 48 'All-Age' songs inspired by stories from the Old Testament, for spreading God's Words all over the world. She lives in England.

Learn English Using Bible Stories!

Hyunju Lee writes an excellent resource to help children learn English using Bible stories. The lessons are entertaining and provide a variety of activities that will help students learn vocabulary and grammar. At the same time, students will learn basic biblical history. The use of a repetitive structure provides familiarity to each lesson so that students can anticipate the next activity. Listening, sentence structure, role play, conversations with partners, and prayer are some of the activities that students will enjoy as they learn and practice English skills. A helpful mini test for each lesson will provide positive feedback to both teacher and student.

Rebecca Scheirer

* Rebecca Scheirer, the Doctor of Ministry, is a Program Administrator for the Doctor of Ministry Program at Wesley Theological Seminary in Washington, D.C., USA. Dr. Scheirer enjoys helping students navigate the difficulties of doctoral studies, and lives in Kensington, Maryland, with her husband.

이 책은 구약성서에 등장하는 주요 인물들과 하나님의 이야기를 영어로 들여다보며, 그 옛날 신앙 선조들의 말과 행동을 통해 우리 자신의 신앙을 되돌아볼 수 있도록 구성한 책입니다. 따라서 이 책이 이끄는 대로 차근차근 따라가다 보면 자신의 신앙을 공고히 할 수 있음은 물론, 글로벌 크리스천에 부응하는 영어 커뮤니케이션 능력도 키울 수 있습니다. 각 과는 다음과 같은 코너들로 구성되어 있습니다.

Who Am I?

이번 과에서 다루는 구약성서 속 인물에 대해 배우게 됩니다.

STEP 1 Listen!

❶ 성서 속 인물을 바로 알려주기보다는 먼저 오디오로 설명을 들으며, 이번 과에서 알아보게 될 인물이 누구인지를 스스로 생각해보는 시간을 가집니다.

❷ 반드시 오디오를 듣고 인물을 추측해본 다음, 아래 스크립트를 확인하세요.

　각 인물에 대한 설명은 각각 두 번씩 들려드립니다.

STEP 2 Speak!

❶ 앞에서 추측해본 인물을 직접 확인해보는 자리입니다. 구약 속 인물에 대한 이야기를 들으며 큰 소리로 여러 번 따라 읽어 보세요.

　각 인물에 대한 설명은 두 번씩 녹음되어 있으며, 처음에는 한 문장씩 듣고 따라읽을 수 있게 문장 단위로 pause를 두었습니다.

❷ 〈Words and Idioms〉를 풀어보며 등장한 표현들의 의미를 생각해 보세요. 무슨 의미인지 바로 생각이 안 나면, 책 맨 뒤의 〈Index Dictionary〉를 활용하면 됩니다.

Grammar Points

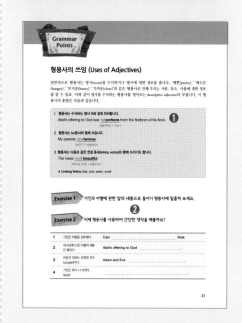

영어 성경책을 바르게 읽고 바르게 이해하기 위해서는 기본적인 영어 문법을 알고 있어야 합니다.

❶ 중학교 교과서에 나오는 기본 문법을 알기 쉽게 간략히 설명해 두었습니다.

❷ 설명을 차근차근 다 읽고 이해한 다음, Exercise를 통해 실생활에 응용할 수 있는 힘을 기르세요.

Let's Talk

영어 성경책을 바르게 읽고 사람들과 신앙을 나누기 위해서는 일상생활에서 흔히 쓰는 표현들을 말할 수 있어야 합니다.

Ⓐ Let's Memorize the Patterns!

❶ 이야기 속에 등장한 유용한 패턴을 엄선해 말하기 훈련을 해보는 자리입니다.

❷ 먼저 패턴과 의미, 활용법을 숙지하세요.

❸ 그런 다음, 오디오를 듣고 예문을 큰소리로 여러 번 따라 읽어 보세요.

🎧 각 문장마다 따라읽을 수 있게 문장길이 만큼 pause가 들어가 있습니다.

Ⓑ Let's Talk: Pair Work

❶ 바로 앞에서 배운 패턴을 이용해 친구들과 실제 대화 연습을 해보는 자리입니다. 빈칸에 원하는 단어를 넣어 친구와 대화해 보세요.

Confession & Prayer

이번 과에서 배운 인물을 떠올리며 자신의 신앙을 고백하고 기도하는 시간을 가져봅니다.

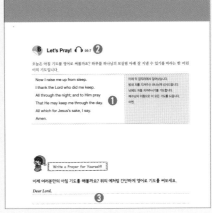

Ⓐ My Confession

❶ 성서 속 인물을 통해 하나님이 전하고자 하신 말씀이 무엇인지에 대해 생각하며, 자신의 신앙을 돌아보는 자리입니다.

❷ 영어로 된 글을 차분히 읽으며 이해해 보세요.

🎧 눈을 감고 오디오를 들으며 다시 한 번 글을 이해해 보세요.

❸ 위의 글속에서 던진 질문에 대해 영어 또는 우리말로 자신의 생각을 써보는 자리입니다.

Ⓑ Let's Pray!

❶ 영어권 기도문을 읽으며 그 의미를 새겨보세요.

❷ 그런 다음 오디오를 듣고, 온 마음을 다해 큰소리로 기도해 보세요.

🎧 기도는 두 번 녹음되어 있으며, 처음에는 한 마디씩 듣고 따라읽을 수 있게 마디 단위로 pause를 두었습니다.

❸ 자신이 하나님께 드리고 싶은 기도를 직접 영어로 적어보는 자리입니다.

A Poem & Song

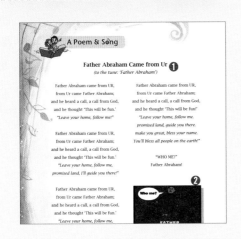

노래를 통해 하나님의 말씀을 기억하고 영어 실력을 키우는 자리입니다.

❶ 가사를 소리 내어 읽으며 그 의미를 새겨보세요.

❷ 그런 다음, 동영상을 보고 들으며 노래를 큰소리로 따라 해 보세요.

🎬 동영상은 www.sheilahamil.co.uk로 접속해 KALEIDOSCOPE OF CHARACTERS 메뉴를 클릭하면 볼 수 있습니다.

Contents

 MP3 파일은 www.kmcedu.or.kr에서 다운로드 받을 수 있습니다.

The Titles of the Bible Books in English

구약의 '창세기'는 영어로 어떻게 쓸까요? 영어 성경을 읽으려면 이처럼 각 책의 영어 명칭을 알아야 합니다. 모든 책의 이름은 대문자로 시작한다는 점에 주의해 다음을 알아두세요!

The Old Testament 구약

Genesis	(Gen.)	창세기	Ecclesiastes	(Eccles.)	전도서
Exodus	(Exod.)	출애굽기	Song of Songs	(Song of Sol.)	아가
Leviticus	(Lev.)	레위기	Isaiah	(Isa.)	이사야
Numbers	(Num.)	민수기	Jeremiah	(Jer.)	예레미야
Deuteronomy	(Deut.)	신명기	Lamentations	(Lam.)	예레미야애가
Joshua	(Josh.)	여호수아	Ezekiel	(Ezek.)	에스겔
Judges	(Judg.)	사사기	Daniel	(Dan.)	다니엘
Ruth	(Ru)	룻기	Hosea	(Hos)	호세아
1 Samuel	(1 Sam.)	사무엘상	Joel	(Jl)	요엘
2 Samuel	(2 Sam.)	사무엘하	Amos	(Am)	아모스
1 Kings	(1 Kgs)	열왕기상	Obadiah	(Obad.)	오바댜
2 Kings	(2 Kgs)	열왕기하	Jonah	(Jon.)	요나
1 Chronicles	(1 Chron.)	역대상	Micah	(Mic.)	미가
2 Chronicles	(2 Chron.)	역대하	Nahum	(Nah.)	나훔
Ezra	(Ezr)	에스라	Habakkuk	(Hab.)	하박국
Nehemiah	(Neh.)	느헤미야	Zephaniah	(Zeph.)	스바냐
Esther	(Est)	에스더	Haggai	(Hag.)	학개
Job	(Jb)	욥기	Zechariah	(Zech.)	스가랴
Psalms	(Ps.)	시편	Malachi	(Mal.)	말라기
Proverbs	(Prov.)	잠언			

The New Testament 신약

Matthew	(Matt.)	마태복음	1 Timothy	(1 Tim.)	디모데전서
Mark	(Mk)	마가복음	2 Timothy	(2 Tim.)	디모데후서
Luke	(Lk)	누가복음	Titus	(Ti)	디도서
John	(Jn)	요한복음	Philemon	(Philem.)	빌레몬서
Acts	(Acts)	사도행전	Hebrews	(Heb.)	히브리서
Romans	(Rom.)	로마서	James	(Jas)	야고보서
1 Corinthians	(1 Cor.)	고린도전서	1 Peter	(1 Pet.)	베드로전서
2 Corinthians	(2 Cor.)	고린도후서	2 Peter	(2 Pet.)	베드로후서
Galatians	(Gal.)	갈라디아서	1 John	(1 Jn)	요한1서
Ephesians	(Eph.)	에베소서	2 John	(2 Jn)	요한2서
Philippians	(Phil.)	빌립보서	3 John	(3 Jn)	요한3서
Colossians	(Col.)	골로새서	Jude	(Jude)	유다서
1 Thessalonians	(1 Thess.)	데살로니가전서	Revelations	(Rev.)	요한계시록
2 Thessalonians	(2 Thess.)	데살로니가후서			

* 괄호 안은 약자

The First Man in the World

So God created man in His own image; in the image of God He created him; male and female He created them. (Gen. 1:27) 📖

STEP 1 Listen!

오디오를 듣고 말하고 있는 인물이 누구인지 알아맞혀 보세요.

A

🎧 01-1

Who am I?

B

🎧 01-2

Who am I?

STEP 2 Speak!

오디오를 듣고 큰소리로 따라 읽어 보세요.

  01-3

 Adam: The First Man

Adam means 'earth' or 'earthy.'

He was the first man.

He was created[1] by God on the sixth day of creation.[2]

He was born when "in the beginning God created the heavens and the earth." (Gen. 1:1)

He lived "in the garden of Eden." (Gen. 2:8)

He was given dominion[3] over the animals.

He had three sons: Cain, Abel and Seth.

He got in trouble because he gave in to[4] temptation.[5]

Words and Idioms Consult the index dictionary if needed.

1 create: to make something new or original that did not exist before 창조하다

2 creation:

3 dominion:

4 give in to:

5 temptation:

Eve: Adam's Wife and Suitable Helper (Gen. 2:21)

Eve means 'mother of all living.'

She was created from her husband's rib.[1]

She lived in "the garden in Eden" (Gen. 2:8) with Adam.

She also had three sons: Cain, Abel and Seth.

She also got in trouble[2] because she gave in to temptation.

She listened to the serpent[3] and questioned[4] God's command.[5]

She and her husband were thrown[6] out of their home place, the Garden of Eden.

| Words and Idioms | Consult the index dictionary if needed.

1 rib: one of the 12 pairs of curved bones that surround your chest 갈비뼈

2 get in trouble:

3 serpent:

4 question (v.):

5 command:

6 throw:

| Think about It! | Talk about Adam and Eve. Who are they?

단어의 기본 순서 (Basic Word Order)

영어 문장을 이루는 가장 기초적인 요소들을 알아볼까요? 다음과 같이 주어와 동사로 시작하는 구조가 바로 영어 문장의 가장 기본적인 순서입니다.

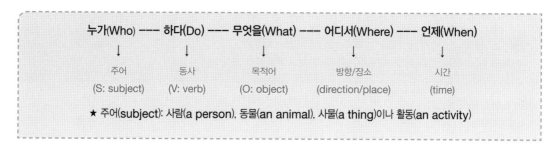

앞에 나온 내용 중에서 몇 문장만 골라 단어의 순서를 살펴볼까요?

Adam means 'earth' or 'earthy.'
 S   V   O

He lived in the Garden of Eden.
 S   V   place

She listened to the serpent and questioned God's command.
 S   V1   O1   V2   O2

▶ V1 listened to는 두 단어이므로 엄밀히 말해 동사구입니다.
   V2 questioned의 주어는 앞에 나온 She로 주어가 같기 때문에 생략되었습니다.

 **Exercise** 아담과 하와에 관한 앞의 내용으로 돌아가 각 문장의 단어 순서를 위와 같이 표시해 보세요.

A Let's Memorize the Patterns! 🎧 01-5

- 주어 + was/were born in + 장소 ~에서 태어났다
  - ▶ 태어난 때는 과거이므로 항상 be동사의 과거형을 써야 합니다.

- 주어 + live (be living) in/at + 장소 ~에서 산다(살고 있다)
  - ▶ 현재 살고 있는 곳을 말할 때는 현재형 혹은 현재진행형을 씁니다.

I was born in Seoul.
나는 서울에서 태어났다.

Hyunmi **was born in** Busan, Korea.
현미는 한국의 부산에서 태어났다. ▶ 지명이 두 개일 때는 크기가 작은 지명부터 먼저 씁니다.

I live (am living) in Busan.
나는 부산에서 산다(살고 있다).

He **lives in** the country with his parents.
그는 부모와 시골에서 산다.

B Let's Talk: Pair Work

두 명씩 한 조를 만들어 보세요. 그런 후 다음에 제시된 문장을 사용하여 서로 영어로 대화해
보세요.

Partner A Where were you born?

Partner B I was born in _____. How about you?

Partner A I was born in _____. Where are you living now?

Partner B I live (am living) in _____.

Are you still living in _____?

Partner A Yes, I live (am living) in _____.

A My Confession 01-6

The Lord God commanded the man, "You are free to eat from any tree in the garden; but you must not eat from the tree of the knowledge of good and evil, for when you eat of it you will surely die." (Gen. 2:16-17) But Eve listened to the snake's words and disobeyed God's command. She also gave Adam some fruit and let him eat it. Do you know what happened after Adam and Eve ate some fruit? Share your idea with group members and write down your idea in English if you can.

여호와 하나님이 그 사람에게 명하여 이르시되 "동산 각종 나무의 열매는 네가 임의로 먹되 선악을 알게 하는 나무의 열매는 먹지 말라. 네가 먹는 날에는 반드시 죽으리라" 하셨습니다.(창세기 2:16-17) 하지만 하와는 뱀의 말을 듣고 하나님의 명령에 복종하지 않았습니다. 뿐만 아니라 하와는 아담에게도 열매를 주어 먹게 하였습니다. 아담과 하와가 열매를 먹은 후 어떤 일이 일어났나요? 다른 친구들과 이야기를 나누어 본 후 가능하면 여러분의 생각을 영어로 써보세요.

 영어로 쓰기가 힘들다면 우리말로 써도 괜찮습니다.

B **Let's Pray!** 🎧 01-7

오늘은 영어로 기도하는 첫 날입니다. 다음의 기도문은 잠자리에 들기 전 미국 아이들이 어릴 때부터 외워온 전통적인 기도문입니다. 우리도 다가오는 한 주 동안 잠자리에 들기 전 이 영어 기도문을 외워 볼까요?

Dear Lord,

Now I lay me down to sleep.

I pray thee, Lord, thy child to keep;

Thy love to guard me through the night

And wake me in the morning light.

사랑의 주님,

이제 저는 잠자리에 듭니다.

주님, 당신의 어린 양을 지켜주소서.

당신의 사랑으로 저를 밤새 지켜주시고,

아침의 빛 안에서 깨어나게 하소서.

★ thy: your의 고어, thee: you의 고어

 Write a Prayer for Yourself!

이제 여러분의 잠자리 기도를 써볼까요? 위의 예처럼 간단하게 영어로 기도를 써보세요.

Dear Lord,

Amen.

The Crafty Serpent

The crafty serpent said to Eve,
"Why not eat of the big fruit tree?
There's no harm go on and eat!
Don't stop!"

So she ate, it tasted sweet
said, "Adam, come and have a piece.
It's so scrummy to eat, I cannot
stop!"

God walked by in the cool of the day,
and they hid from him as he walked
that way!
Then he knew they disobeyed!
He said, "Stop!"

*"HAVE YOU BOTH EATEN FROM THE
TREE THAT
I COMMANDED YOU NOT TO EAT
FROM?"*

"It wasn't my fault it was Eve to blame!
She's the one who brought me shame!"
"No t'was the snake!" said she, and God
said, "Stop!"

Out of the garden they did go,
to work on the land in the rain and
snow,
all because they ate, and didn't
STOP!
STOP!
STOP!
STOP!

"There's no harm, go on eat! DON'T STOP!"

used with permission www.sheilahamil.co.uk

02

The First Murderer in the World

Adam lay with his wife Eve, and she became pregnant and gave birth to Cain. "With the help of the LORD I have brought forth a man." Later she gave birth to his brother Abel.

(Gen. 4:1-2)

Who Am I?

STEP 1 Listen!

오디오를 듣고 말하고 있는 인물이 누구인지 알아맞혀 보세요.

A

🎧 02-1

Who am I?   🖉 _____

B

🎧 02-2

🖉 _____   Who am I?

A | My parents are very famous as the first couple in the world. I was their firstborn child. I was a farmer. I 'brought some of the fruits of the soil as an offering' to God, but my offering to God was rejected. I killed my younger brother in jealousy and anger because God only accepted his offering. I was condemned to be a wanderer after I murdered him in the field. Who am I?

B | My parents are very famous, too. I was a shepherd. I had an elder brother. I offered to God, 'fat portions from some of the firstborn of his flock.' (Gen. 4:4) My elder brother was jealous of me because God had only regard on my offering, not my brother's. I was murdered by my brother. After that, I was famous for how I died. Who am I?

STEP 2 `Speak!`

오디오를 듣고 큰소리로 따라 읽어 보세요.

  02-3

 Cain: The First Murderer[1]

His parents are very famous as the first couple in the world.

He was their firstborn[2] child. He was a farmer.

He 'brought some of the fruits of the soil as an offering[3]' to God (Gen. 4:3), but his offering to God was rejected.[4]

He killed his younger brother in jealousy and anger because God only accepted his younger brother's offering.

He was condemned[5] to be a wanderer[6] after he murdered his brother in the field.

┌─────────────────────┐
│ **Words and Idioms** │ Consult the index dictionary if needed.
└─────────────────────┘

1 murderer: someone who commits murder 살인자

2 firstborn:

3 offering:

4 reject:

5 condemn:

6 wanderer:

Abel: The Pitiful Younger Brother

His parents are very famous,[1] too.

He was a shepherd.[2]

His offering to God was 'fat portions[3] from some of the firstborn of his flock[4].' (Gen. 4:4)

His elder brother was jealous of[5] him because God had only regard[6] on his offering, not his brother's.

He was murdered by his brother.

After that, he was famous for how he died.

Words and Idioms Consult the index dictionary if needed.

1 famous: known about by many people in many places 유명한

2 shepherd:

3 portion:

4 flock:

5 jealous of:

6 regard:

Think about It! Talk about Cain and Abel. Who are they?

형용사의 쓰임 (Uses of Adjectives)

일반적으로 형용사는 명사(noun)를 수식하거나 명사에 대한 정보를 줍니다. '예쁜(pretty),' '배고픈 (hungry),' '무거운(heavy),' '가까운(close)'과 같은 형용사로 인해 우리는 사람, 장소, 사물에 대한 정보를 알 수 있죠. 이와 같이 명사를 수식하는 형용사를 영어로는 descriptive adjective라 부릅니다. 이 형용사의 용법은 다음과 같습니다.

---

1. 형용사는 수식하는 명사 바로 앞에 위치합니다.

   Abel's offering to God was <u>fat</u> **portions** from the firstborn of his flock.

   adjective + noun

2. 형용사는 be동사와 함께 쓰입니다.

   My parents <u>are</u> **famous**.

   be동사 + adjective

3. 형용사는 다음과 같은 연결 동사(linking verbs)와 함께 쓰이기도 합니다.

   The roses <u>look</u> **beautiful**.

   linking verb + adjective

   ★ **Linking Verbs:** feel, look, seem, smell

Exercise 1 가인과 아벨에 관한 앞의 내용으로 돌아가 형용사에 밑줄쳐 보세요.

Exercise 2 이제 형용사를 사용하여 간단한 영작을 해볼까요?

1	가인은 아벨을 질투했다.	Cain _____ Abel.
2	하나님께 드린 아벨의 제물은 좋았다.	Abel's offering to God _____ .
3	아담과 하와는 유명한 부부 (couple)이다.	Adam and Eve _____ .
4	가인은 화가 나 보였다. (look)	_____ .

 A **Let's Memorize the Patterns!** 🎧 02-5

> • 주어 + be famous as + 직업/직위 ~로서 유명하다
> ▶ as는 '~로서'의 뜻으로 그 다음에 주로 직업이나 직위 등 현재의 상태를 씁니다.
>
> • 주어 + be famous for ~로 유명해지다
> ▶ for 다음에는 천재성이나 아름다움 등 유명하게 된 이유가 나와야 합니다.
> ★ for 다음에는 명사, 명사구(the Tree of Knowledge), 혹은 절(how he died)을 써도 됩니다.

Adam and Eve are very famous as the first couple in the world.
아담과 하와는 세계에서 첫 번째 부부로 매우 유명하다. (~로서)

Cain is famous as the first murderer in the world.
가인은 세계에서 최초의 살인자로 유명하다. (~로)

The Garden of Eden is famous for the Tree of Knowledge.
에덴동산은 선악과로 유명하다. (~로)

Abel is famous for how he died.
아벨은 어떻게 죽었는지로 유명하다. (~로)

 B **Let's Talk: Pair Work**

두 명씩 한 조를 만들어 보세요. 그런 후 다음에 제시된 문장을 사용하여 서로 영어로 대화해 보세요.

Partner A He(She) is famous as _____.

Partner B I've never heard about it. Is he(she) really famous as _____?

Partner A Yeah, he(she) is especially famous for _____.

Partner B If I have a chance, I will go and see his(her) works.

Partner A That's a great idea!

> **Substitution Practices** • an artist-his(her) creativity | a singer-(his/her) high pitched tone | painter-beautiful colors | an actor(actress)-his(her) fantastic body shape | a scholar-(his/her) intelligence | a dancer-advanced techniques

Confession & Prayer

 A **My Confession** 🎧 02-6

After Cain killed his brother in the field, God said to him, "Where is your brother Abel?"(Gen. 4:9) To this question, Cain answered, "I don't know. Am I my brother's keeper?"(Gen. 4:9) Because Cain did not confess his sin, and he even lied to God, he was sent away and became a restless wanderer.(Gen. 4:12) Sometimes you might have chances to hide your faults and even feel the desire to tell lies. If you are in this situation, what are you going to do? What do you think is the best way in the eyes of God? Share your idea with other group members and write down your idea in English if you can.

가인이 들판에서 동생을 죽인 후, 하나님이 그에게 물었습니다. "네 아우 아벨이 어디 있느냐?"(창세기 4:9) 이에 가인이 대답했습니다. "내가 알지 못하나이다. 내가 내 아우를 지키는 자이니까?"(창세기 4:9) 가인이 자신의 죄를 고백하지 않고, 더구나 하나님께 거짓으로 고했기 때문에 그는 쫓겨나 유랑하는 신세가 되었습니다.(창세기 4:12) 때때로 여러분은 자신의 잘못을 숨기고 거짓말을 하고 싶은 기회를 만날지도 모릅니다. 이런 상황에 처한다면 여러분은 어떻게 할 건가요? 하나님의 눈으로 볼 때 최선의 길은 무엇인가요? 다른 친구들과 이야기를 나누어 본 후 여러분의 생각을 가능하면 영어로 써보세요.

 영어로 쓰기가 힘들다면 우리말로 써도 괜찮습니다.

B Let's Pray! 🎧 02-7

우리도 가인처럼 분노를 느낄 때가 종종 있습니다. 이렇게 화가 날 때 화를 누그러뜨리는 기도를 해보세요. 다음은 어린아이가 자신의 분노를 억누르게 해달라는 내용의 기도입니다. 가능하면 외워보는 것도 좋겠죠?

Dear God,

We get angry at so many things–our teachers, work, friends and families.

Lord, help us to pray to you more when we are angry.

Teach us to be more tolerant of others.

Let us remember that harsh words and violence are not the answer.

Calm us with your peace and love.

Amen.

사랑의 주님,

너무 많은 것들 때문에 화가 납니다. 선생님, 일, 친구, 가족 때문에요.

하나님, 화가 날 때면 더 많이 기도할 수 있도록 도와주세요.

다른 사람들의 행동을 참을 수 있도록 가르쳐 주세요.

거친 말과 폭력이 답이 아님을 기억하게 해주세요.

주님의 평화와 사랑으로 우리의 마음을 평안하게 해주세요.

아멘.

Write a Prayer for Yourself!

이제 여러분이 화가 났을 때 할 수 있는 기도를 써볼까요? 위의 예처럼 간단하게 영어로 기도를 써보세요.

Dear God,

Amen.

Cain and Abel

(to the tune 'This Old Man')

Eve bore Cain, her first born son,
Abel was her second one.
With a knick knack paddy whack,
she was not alone.
Adam helped her in the home.

Cain and Abel, brothers two,
fine and tall and strong they grew.
With a knick knack paddy whack,
even when they'd grown,
they had strengths to call their own.

Cain was 'able', he grew seed;
he was gifted, yes indeed.
With a knick knack paddy whack,
gave God what he'd grown.
Abel gave fat meat on bone.

Abel's gift was loved the more,
sin came crouching at Cain's door!
With a knick knack paddy whack,
jealousy is sin.
So he did his brother in!

"Where is Abel, is he alive?"
"I don't know," said Cain who lied.
With a knick knack paddy whack
"Listen hear the sound
Abel's blood cries from the ground!"

Abel's death was cold and slick.
What was done Cain could not fix!
With a knick knack paddy whack,
he ran away from God.
Off he fled to a land called Nod!

used with permission www.sheilahamil.co.uk

03

The Righteous Man in the Corrupted World

Noah was a righteous man, blameless among the people of his time,

and he walked with God. (Gen. 4:9) 📖

Who Am I?

STEP 1 Listen!

오디오를 듣고 말하고 있는 인물이 누구인지 알아맞혀 보세요.

A

🎧 03-1

Who am I?

✏️

B

🎧 03-2

Who am I?

✏️

A | I was a righteous man. I always walked with God when everyone else became selfish and mean. I listened to God's specific instructions and built a large boat, which took many years. It rained a lot soon after I finished building my work. I had to take care of all kinds of animals for nearly six months. When the sun came out, my family and all kinds of animals were told to go out from the ark. I was thankful that God saved my family, so I built an altar to please Him. Who am I?

B | I was displeased to see people living their lives apart from me. I tried to speak to them in many different ways, but they would not listen. I could not stand them. So I decided to send a deep flood and destroy everything living on earth. I ordered Noah, the righteous man, to build an ark and gather two of every living creature in that ark. After the flood was over, I set a beautiful rainbow in the sky and made a promise never again to destroy the world with flood waters. Who am I?

STEP 2 Speak!

오디오를 듣고 큰소리로 따라 읽어 보세요.

 03-3

 ## Noah: The Righteous[1] Man

He was a righteous man. (Gen. 6:9)

He always walked with God when everyone else became selfish and mean.[2]

He listened to God's specific[3] instructions[4] and built a large boat, which took many years.

It rained a lot soon after he finished building his work.

He had to take care of[5] all kinds of animals for nearly six months.

When the sun came out, his family and all kinds of animals were told to go out from the ark.[6]

He was thankful God saved his family, so he built an altar[7] to please Him.

| Words and Idioms | Consult the index dictionary if needed.

1 righteous: morally good or correct 의로운

2 mean: **3** specific:

4 instruction: **5** take care of:

6 ark: **7** altar:

 **B** 🎧 03-4

 ## God: The Covenant¹ Giver

God was displeased² to see people living their lives apart from³ Him.

He tried to speak to them in many different ways, but they would not listen.

He could not stand⁴ them, so He decided to send a deep flood and destroy⁵ everything living on earth.

He ordered Noah, the righteous man, to build an ark and gather⁶ two of every living creature in that ark.

After the flood⁷ was over, He set a beautiful rainbow in the sky, and it was a sign⁸ of a promise that God would never destroy the world with flood waters again.

Words and Idioms Consult the index dictionary if needed.

1 covenant: a formal agreement or promise 언약

2 displeased: ....

3 apart from: ....

4 stand: ....

5 destroy: ....

6 gather: ....

7 flood: ....

8 sign: ....

Think about It! Talk about Noah. Who is he?

빈도부사 (Adverbs of Frequency)

빈도부사는 always/usually/often/sometimes/seldom/rarely/never와 같은 단어들을 말합니다. 문장에서 빈도부사의 위치는 다음과 같습니다.

1. Be동사와 함께 쓸 경우

주어 + be +	빈도부사	
Minsu + is +	always / usually / often / sometimes seldom / rarely / never	+ late for class.

민수는 [항상 / 일상적으로 / 자주 / 때때로] 수업에 늦는다.
민수는 [거의 / 좀처럼 / 결코] 수업에 늦지 않는다.

2. Be동사를 제외한 일반 동사와 함께 쓸 경우: 주어 + 빈도부사 + 동사

주어 +	빈도부사	+ 동사
Minsu +	always / usually / often / sometimes seldom / rarely / never	+ comes late.

민수는 [항상 / 일상적으로 / 자주 / 때때로] 늦게 온다.
민수는 [거의 / 좀처럼 / 결코] 늦게 오지 않는다.

 Exercise 다음 빈칸에 적절한 빈도부사를 써보세요.

A: Minsu is a very good student.

B: I know. He's ❶_____ late for class.

A: Besides that, he's ❷_____ had his homework done on time.

B: And he ❸_____ makes any noises.

A: He has ❹_____ fought with other students.

B: And he's ❺_____ trying to help his classmates.

A Let's Memorize the Patterns! 🎧 03-5

- 주어 + be glad/pleased to see + 명사 ~를 보니 기쁘다
- 주어 + be sad/displeased to see + 명사 ~를 보니 슬프다

★ glad, sad 대신 다음과 같은 형용사를 써도 됩니다.

afraid 두려운　　disappointed 실망한　　happy 행복한　　lucky 행운인
proud 자랑스러운　sorry 마음이 아픈　　surprised 놀라운

- 주어 + be glad/pleased to see (that) ~ ~가 …한 것을 알고[보니] 기쁘다
- 주어 + be sad/displeased to see (that) ~ ~가 …한 것을 알고[보니] 슬프다

▶ that 뒤에는 〈주어 + 동사〉로 시작되는 완전한 문장을 이어주세요.
★ see 대신 다음과 같은 동사를 써서 말해도 됩니다.

discover 발견하다　find out 발견하다, 알아내다　hear 듣다　learn 알다

I **was glad/pleased to see** him at the meeting.
나는 그를 모임에서 봐서 기뻤다.

I **am sad/displeased to see (that)** my pet Arong is sick.
나는 내 반려동물인 아롱이가 아파서 슬프다.

B Let's Talk: Pair Work

두 명씩 한 조를 만들어 보세요. 그런 후 다음에 제시된 문장을 사용하여 서로 영어로 대화해
보세요.

1	Partner A	I'm ____(good)____ to see you ____(again)____ .
	Partner B	Same here. I'm so ____(happy)____ to see you again!
2	Partner A	Congratulations! I was(am) so ____(happy)____ to hear that you were accepted at Hankuk University.
	Partner B	Thank you! I was so ____(happy)____ to hear that! But now I'm a little ____(worried)____ to think about that I have to move away from my parents.

Confession & Prayer

A My Confession 03-6

In the time when everyone became selfish and mean, Noah and his family always walked with God. He and his family were saved from flood waters because they followed God's words without any doubts. When the flood was over, God gave Noah a promise that he would never again destroy the world. God showed him a rainbow, saying "This is the sign of the covenant I have established between me and all life on earth." (Gen. 9:17) In order to follow Noah, the person of faith in the Bible, what should we do in this world? Share your idea with group members and write down your idea in English if you can.

모든 사람이 이기적이고 비열한 시절에 노아와 그의 가족은 항상 하나님과 함께 동행하였습니다. 이들은 하나님의 말씀을 아무 의심 없이 따랐기 때문에 홍수에서도 살아남았어요. 홍수가 멈추었을 때 하나님은 다시는 세상을 파괴하지 않겠다는 약속을 노아에게 하셨습니다. 하나님은 "내가 나와 땅에 있는 모든 생물 사이에 세운 언약의 증거가 이것이라"(창세기 9:17) 하시며 노아에게 무지개를 보여 주셨습니다. 성경 속 믿음의 사람인 노아를 따르기 위해서 우리는 이 세상에서 어떻게 행동해야 할까요? 다른 친구들과 이야기를 나누어 본 후 여러분의 생각을 가능하면 영어로 써보세요.

 영어로 쓰기가 힘들다면 우리말로 써도 괜찮습니다.

B Let's Pray! 🎧 03-7

하나님은 우리가 잘못할 때 벌을 주는 분이시기도 하지만 이 잘못을 용서하고 감싸주는 분이시기도 합니다. 노아에게 무지개를 보여주시며 하신 약속을 생각하며 모든 것을 주시는 하나님께 감사 기도를 드려봅시다. 우리 주변에서 감사해야 할 일을 생각해 볼까요? 먼저 우리 생활에서 가장 기본적이지만 없어서는 안 될, 음식에 대한 감사의 마음을 식사 전 기도를 통해 전해봅시다. 다음은 하나님께서 주신 음식에 대해 감사하며 쓴 기도입니다.

Great God, Thou Giver of all good. Accept our praise and bless our food. Grace, health, and strength to us afford Through Jesus Christ, our blessed Lord, Amen.	위대하신 하나님, 모든 선한 것을 주시는 하나님. 우리의 칭송을 받으시고 우리의 음식에 축복을 내려주소서. 축복이신 주님, 예수 그리스도를 통해 은총, 건강, 힘을 저희에게 베풀어 주소서. 아멘.

Write a Prayer for Yourself!

이제 여러분만의 식사 전 기도를 써볼까요? 위의 예처럼 간단하게 영어로 기도를 써보세요.

Dear Lord,

Amen.

Two Red Butterflies

(to the tune 'Skip to My Lou')

Two red butterflies fluttering by,
one flew low and one flew high.
They were hurrying, want to know why?
Where were they going that morning?

Two brown monkeys caught my eye,
one was cute; the other was sly.
They were hurrying, want to know why?
Where were they going that morning?

Two grey hippos thundering by,
one was wet; the other was dry.
They were hurrying, want to know why?
Where were they going that morning?

Two yellow lions both drew nigh,
one was bold and one was shy.
They were hurrying, want to know why?
Where were they going that morning?

Two black spiders scurrying by,
one said "Hi!" and the other said "Bye"
They were hurrying, want to know why?
Where were they going that morning?

Two orange tigers raced on by,
one was fierce and one was kind.
They were hurrying, want to know why?
Where were they going that morning?

Two white swans went gliding by,
one was clumsy and one had style.
They were hurrying, want to know why?
Where were they going that morning?

All of the animals, great and small,
were made by God 'cos He loved them all.
They were listening to His call
to come to the Ark that morning.

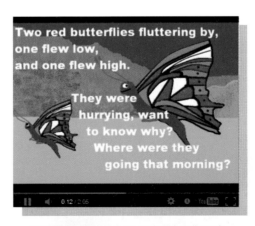

used with permission www.sheilahamil.co.uk

04

Father of Many Nations

No longer will you be called Abram: your name will be Abraham, for I have made you

a father of many nations. (Gen. 17:5) 📖

STEP 1 Listen!

오디오를 듣고 말하고 있는 인물이 누구인지 알아맞혀 보세요.

A

🎧 04-1

Who am I?

B

🎧 04-2

Who am I?

Script

A | My name means "father of many nations." My name was changed when God made a covenant with me. I was born in Ur, but I moved into Egypt because of the famine. I saved my nephew, Lot's life because I asked God to save a few righteous people before destroying Sodom. When I was 86 years old, my first son, Ishmael was born by Hagar, a slave-girl. Almost 14 years later, I had another son, Isaac by my legal wife, Sarah. I was asked by God to sacrifice Isaac, so I prepared to sacrifice him. But God sent a ram to take Isaac's place. As God promised, I came to have a lot of descendants and became a father of Israel. Who am I?

B | My name means "princess." My name was changed when God made a covenant with my husband and me. My husband's name is Abraham. I really wanted to have a child, but I could not. So I pushed Abraham into having a child by Hagar. When I was 89 years old, God promised me to give a child. At first, I could not believe it because I was too old to have a baby. But God's promise came true. I had my first child, Isaac, when I was about 90 years old. Who am I?

STEP 2 Speak!

오디오를 듣고 큰소리로 따라 읽어 보세요.

  04-3

 ### Abraham: The Father of Many Nations[1]

Abraham means "father of many nations."

His name was changed[2] when God made a covenant with him.

He was born in Ur, but he moved into Egypt because of the famine.

He saved his nephew, Lot's life because he asked God to save a few righteous people

before destroying Sodom.

When he was 86 years old, his first son, Ishmael was born by Hagar, a slave-girl.

Almost 14 years later, he had another son, Isaac by his legal[3] wife, Sarah.

He was asked by God to sacrifice[4] Isaac.

He prepared[5] to sacrifice his son, but God sent a ram[6] to take Isaac's place.[7]

As God promised, he came to have a lot of descendants[8] and became a father of Israel.

| Words and Idioms | Consult the index dictionary if needed.

1 nation: a country that has its own land and government 국가

2 change:

3 legal:

4 sacrifice:

5 prepare:

6 ram:

7 take someone's place:

8 descendant:

04-4

 Sarah: The Wife of Abraham

Sarah means "princess."

Her name was changed when God made a covenant with her and her husband.

Her husband's name is Abraham.

She wanted to have a child, but she could not.

So she pushed Abraham into having a child by Hagar, a slave[1]-girl.

When she was 89 years old, God promised her to give a child.

At first, she could not believe it because she was too old to have a baby.

God's promise came true.[2]

She had her first child, Isaac, when she was about 90 years old.

Words and Idioms Consult the index dictionary if needed.

1 slave: someone who belongs by law to another person as their property and has to obey them and work for them 노예

2 come true:

Think about It! Talk about Abraham. Who is he?

동사의 종류 (Verbs 1): 자동사와 타동사

문장에서 동사의 역할은 매우 중요합니다. 주어의 동작이나 상태를 나타내기 때문이죠. 이와 같은 동사는 목적어(object)를 취하지 않는 자동사(verb intransitive)와 목적어를 취하는 타동사(verb transitive)로 크게 분류됩니다.

---

1. **자동사(Verb Intransitive)**

   〈주어 + 동사〉 형태의 문장에서 쓰이며, '부사' 및 '전치사를 동반한 부사구'가 함께 쓰이는 경우가 많죠.

   <u>Abraham</u> <u>moved</u> <u>into Egypt</u>.
   　주어　　자동사　전치사 + 명사(장소를 나타내는 부사구)

   ★ 구(phrase): 주어와 동사를 포함하지 않은 단어 무리

2. **타동사(Verb Transitive)**

   〈주어 + 동사 + 목적어〉 형태의 문장에서 사용됩니다.

   <u>Abraham</u> <u>means</u> <u>"father of many nations."</u>
   　주어　　타동사　　　　목적어

다음 문장에서 밑줄 친 동사가 자동사인지, 타동사인지 구별해 보세요. 더불어 위에서 제시한 것과 같이 <주어 + 동사 + 부사구>, <주어 + 동사 + 목적어>의 순서로 문장 구조를 파악해 보세요.

1 God <u>created</u> man in his own image.

2 Adam and Eve <u>lived</u> in the Garden of Eden.

3 Cain <u>killed</u> his younger brother in jealousy and anger.

4 Noah always <u>walked</u> with God.

5 It <u>rained</u> a lot.

6 God <u>set</u> a beautiful rainbow in the sky.

A Let's Memorize the Patterns! 04-5

• 주어 + ask + 사람 + a question ~에게 질문하다
• 주어 + ask + 사람 + for 명사 ~에게 …을 요구하다
• 주어 + ask + 사람 + to 동사원형 ~에게 …을 해달라고 요구하다

Can/May I ask you a question?

질문 하나 해도 될까요? ▶ can은 친구처럼 편한 관계일 때 사용하고, may는 선생님에게 정중하게 이야기할 경우 등에 사용합니다.

Can/May I ask you a personal question? 사적인 질문을 해도 될까요?

▶ 외국 사람들은 나이, 결혼 유무처럼 사적인 질문을 하지 않습니다. 하지만 꼭 하고 싶은 경우에는 이와 같이 정중하게 물어보세요.

Can/May I ask you for a favor?

부탁 하나 해도 될까요?

I have a big favor to ask you.

꼭 부탁드릴 것이 있습니다. ▶ big favor는 큰 부탁이 아니라 중요한 부탁입니다.

Can I ask you to help me with my homework?

숙제 좀 도와줄 수 있어요?

Mom always asks me to pick up the phone.

엄마는 항상 나한테 전화 받으라고 하셔.

B Let's Talk: Pair Work

두 명씩 한 조를 만들어 보세요. 그런 후 다음에 제시된 문장을 사용하여 서로 영어로 대화해 보세요.

1	Partner A	Can I ask a (personal) question?	Partner B Sure.
	Partner A		
	Partner B		
2	Partner A	Could I ask you a favor?	
	Partner B	Of course!	
	Partner A	Please	

Confession & Prayer

 A **My Confession** 🎧 04-6

Abraham and Sarah wanted very much to have children, but they thought they were too old. Sarah even laughed when a visitor told her she would have a child (Gen. 18:12). Then she found out that the visitor was God and God's promise came true. She had a son when she was 90 years old. Sometimes we should wait for a long time until God's promises come true. It can be easier for us to give up hope. But God is always with us and fulfills His promises. Do you believe this? Share your idea with group members and write down your idea in English if you can.

아브라함과 사라는 아이를 매우 갖고 싶어 했지만 자신들이 너무 늙었다고 생각했습니다. 손님이 와서 그녀가 아이를 갖게 될 것이라고 말하자 사라는 웃기까지 했습니다.(창세기 18:12) 얼마 후 사라는 그 손님이 여호와 하나님인 것을 알았고 하나님의 언약은 실현되었습니다. 사라는 아흔 살에 아들을 낳았습니다. 때때로 우리는 하나님의 언약이 실현되기까지 오래 기다려야만 합니다. 희망을 포기하는 편이 쉬울 수도 있습니다. 하지만 하나님은 항상 우리와 함께 계시며 당신의 약속을 실행하십니다. 여러분은 이를 믿습니까? 다른 친구들과 이야기를 나누어 본 후 여러분의 생각을 가능하면 영어로 써보세요.

 영어로 쓰기가 힘들다면 우리말로 써도 괜찮습니다.

B **Let's Pray!** 🎧 04-7

하나님은 항상 우리와 함께 계십니다. 하나님께서 항상 우리 안에 계시기를 바라는 내용을 담은 16세기의 기도문을 한번 볼까요?

God be in my head,	하나님 제 머리 안에 계셔주세요.
And in my understanding;	잘 이해할 수 있게요.
God be in my eyes,	하나님 제 눈 안에 계셔주세요.
And in my looking;	잘 볼 수 있게요.
God be in my mouth,	하나님 제 입 안에 계셔주세요.
And in my speaking;	잘 말할 수 있게요.
God be in my heart,	하나님 제 마음 안에 계셔주세요.
And in my thinking;	잘 생각할 수 있게요.
God be at my end,	하나님 제 목적지에 계셔주세요.
And at my departing.	잘 출발할 수 있게요.

 Write a Prayer for Yourself!

위의 기도문은 간단하면서도 재미있게 쓰인 기도문입니다. 여러분도 위의 구조에 맞춰 하고 싶은 기도를 해볼까요?

God be

And

God be

And

God be

And

Father Abraham Came from Ur

(to the tune: 'Father Abraham')

Father Abraham came from UR,
from Ur came Father Abraham;
and he heard a call, a call from God,
and he thought 'This will be fun.'
"Leave your home, follow me!"

Father Abraham came from UR,
from Ur came Father Abraham;
and he heard a call, a call from God,
and he thought 'This will be fun.'
"Leave your home, follow me,
promised land, I'll guide you there!"

Father Abraham came from UR,
from Ur came Father Abraham;
and he heard a call, a call from God,
and he thought 'This will be fun.'
"Leave your home, follow me,
promised land, I'll guide you there,
make you great, bless your name!"

Father Abraham came from UR,
from Ur came Father Abraham;
and he heard a call, a call from God,
and he thought 'This will be fun!'
"Leave your home, follow me.
promised land, guide you there.
make you great, bless your name.
You'll bless all people on the earth!"

"WHO ME?"
Father Abraham!

used with permission www.sheilahamil.co.uk

Mini Test

Class _____   Name _____

A Dictation Test 🎧 04-8

■ 오디오를 듣고 단어를 받아쓰세요. 단어는 각각 세 번씩 들려드립니다.

01 _____   02 _____   03 _____

04 _____   05 _____   06 _____

07 _____   08 _____   09 _____

10 _____   11 _____   12 _____

■ 오디오를 듣고 다음 문장을 받아쓰세요. 문장은 세 번 들려드립니다.

13 N_____ _____ _____ _____ _____ _____ _____ _____ _____

_____ _____ _____.

B Reading Comprehension Test

■ 다음 인물에 적합한 설명을 아래 보기에서 골라 쓰세요.

01 Adam _____   02 Eve _____

03 Cain _____   04 Abel _____

05 Noah _____   06 God _____

07 Abraham _____   08 Sarah _____

(a) I listened to God's specific instructions and built a large boat.

(b) I killed my younger brother in anger because God only accepted his offering.

(c) My name means 'earth' or 'earthy.'

(d) I had my first child when I was about 90 years old.

(e) I was famous for how I died.

(f) I listened to the serpent and questioned God's command.

(g) I set a beautiful rainbow when the flood was over.

(h) I was asked by God to sacrifice my son.

 **Grammar Test**

01 다음 문장 중에서 단어의 기본 순서가 틀린 것은?

(a) She listened to the serpent.

(b) She also got trouble in.

(c) She had three sons.

(d) He lived in the garden in Eden.

02 다음 문장 중 밑줄 친 단어가 형용사가 아닌 것은?

(a) My parents are <u>famous</u>.

(b) The roses looks <u>beautiful</u>.

(c) Minsu is <u>sometimes</u> late for class.

(d) I had an <u>elder</u> brother.

03 다음 두 문장에 빈도부사 always를 넣어보세요.

(a) Minsu   is   tired.

(b) Younghee   looks   happy.

04 다음 문장의 동사가 자동사인지 타동사인지 써보세요.

(a) It <u>rained</u> a lot.

(b) Abraham <u>moved</u> into another place.

(c) God <u>loves</u> me.

05 다음 질문에 적절한 대답을 써보세요.

A: Where were you born?

B: _____

Activity ❶

Let's Be Voice Actors!

다음 이야기는 에덴동산에서의 아담과 하와의 이야기입니다. 여러분이 라디오 드라마를 연기하는 성우가 되어 다음 이야기를 읽어보세요. 등장인물의 감정선을 잘 분석해 마치 자신이 그 인물이 된 것처럼 실감나게 연기해야 해요!

- 밑줄 친 부분에는 여러분이 직접 대사를 만들어 연기하세요.
- 괄호 안에는 등장인물의 감정이 어떤지 간단하게 감정을 나타내는 형용사를 써보세요.

ADAM AND EVE

Place: the Garden of Eden
Characters: Narrator, God, the serpent, Adam, Eve

Narrator: God planted a garden in a place called Eden. The garden was filled with many beautiful plants. God put Adam in the garden to take care of it.

God: (   ) You may eat the fruit from any tree in the garden except one. Do not eat from that tree. If you eat from the tree of knowing good and evil, you will die.

Adam: _____

Narrator: God thought it was not good for Adam to be alone. So He made a woman from Adam's rib. God brought the woman to Adam and he was very pleased. Adam and Eve lived happily in the garden.

- 아담과 하와의 행복한 순간이 담긴 대사를 만들어 보세요.

Adam: (   ) _____

Eve: (   ) _____

58

Narrator:	One day Eve met the serpent. The serpent was a clever creature.
The serpent:	(　　　　) Did God really tell you not to eat fruit?
Eve:	(　　　　) Of course we may eat fruit from all the trees except one. If we eat that fruit, we will die.
The serpent:	(　　　　) You will not! If you eat it, you will be like God. You will know good and evil.
Narrator:	The fruit looked fresh and tasty, so Eve took and ate it. Then she went to Adam and gave the fruit to him. Adam ate it, too. Suddenly they saw that they had no clothes, so they made clothes from fig leaves. They hid when they heard the voice of God.
God:	Adam, Where are you?
Adam:	(　　　　) We're hiding because we are naked and afraid.
God:	(　　　　) Did you eat fruit from the tree I said not to eat?
Adam:	(　　　　) The woman you made to be my helper, she gave the fruit to me and I ate it.
God:	(to Eve) What have you done?
Eve:	(　　　　) The serpent tricked me, and I ate it.
God:	(to the serpent) From now on, you will crawl on your belly in the dust.
Narrator:	The serpent fell silent on the ground and slithered away.
God:	(to Adam and Eve) You disobeyed Me, so you shall work very hard for your daily bread. You will die and turn back into dust.
Narrator:	God made clothes for them and sent them out of the garden of Eden, never to return again. Behind them he placed an angel with a flaming sword to guard the entrance to Eden.

■ 에덴동산에서 쫓겨나는 아담과 하와의 모습을 상상하며 대사를 만들어 보세요.

Adam: (　　　　) _____

Eve: (　　　　) _____

- THE END -

05

The Son in Abraham's Old Age

Sarah said, "God has brought me laughter, and everyone who hears about this will laugh with me." And she added "Who would have said to Abraham that Sarah would nurse children? Yet I have borne him a son in his old age." (Gen. 21: 6-7)

Who Am I?

STEP 1 Listen!

오디오를 듣고 말하고 있는 인물이 누구인지 알아맞혀 보세요.

A

🎧 05-1

Who am I?

✏️

B

🎧 05-2

✏️

Who am I?

Script

A | My name means "he laughs." I was born when my parents were very old. I was almost sacrificed by my father, but God sent a ram to take my place. I was married to Rebekah. I had twin sons named Jacob and Esau. I loved my first son, Esau, while my wife's favorite was the younger brother, Jacob. When I was old and could not see well, I was tricked by my wife, Rebekah, and my son, Jacob. I gave Jacob the blessing meant for Esau. Who am I?

B | I was a sister of Laban. I was sought out by a servant to be Isaac's wife. I was childless for twenty years after I got married. I was the mother of twins. Because I tricked my husband into giving Jacob the blessing meant for Esau, some people might think that I was a schemer. But I was just concerned about my younger son. I always believed God's words, "the older will serve the younger." (Gen. 25:23) I urged my favorite son, Jacob, to flee Esau's fury and never saw him again. Who am I?

STEP 2 Speak!

오디오를 듣고 큰소리로 따라 읽어 보세요.

 ## Isaac: The Son in Abraham's Old Age

Isaac means "he laughs."

He was born when his parents were very old.

He was almost sacrificed by his father, but God sent a ram to take his place.

He was married to Rebekah.

He had twin[1] sons named Jacob and Esau.

He loved his first son, Esau, while his wife's favorite was the younger brother, Jacob.

When he was old and could not see well, he was tricked[2] by his wife, Rebekah, and his son, Jacob.

He gave Jacob the blessing[3] meant for Esau.

| Words and Idioms | Consult the index dictionary if needed.

1 twin: one of two children born at the same time to the same mother 쌍둥이

2 trick:

3 blessing:

05-4

 Rebekah: Isaac's Wife

She was a sister of Laban.

She was sought[1] out by a servant to be Isaac's wife.

She was childless[2] for twenty years after she got married.

She was the mother of twins.

She tricked her husband into giving Jacob the blessing meant for Esau, so sometimes she has been considered to be a schemer.[3]

She might want to say that she was just concerned about[4] her younger son, and she always believed God's words, "the older will serve the younger." (Gen. 25:23)

She urged[5] her favorite son, Jacob, to flee[6] Esau's fury[7] and never saw him again.

| Words and Idioms | Consult the index dictionary if needed.

1 seek: to ask for something or try to get something 찾다, 추구하다

2 childless:

3 schemer:

4 concerned about:

5 urge:

6 flee:

7 fury:

Pop Quiz!!

Laban은 Rebekah의 오빠이며, Rebekah의 아버지는 Abraham의 동생인 Nahor입니다. 그렇다면 Abraham과 Rebekah의 관계는 어떻게 될까요?

동사의 종류 (Verbs 2): 완전 자동사와 불완전 자동사

자동사는 완전 자동사(Verb Intransitive)와 불완전 자동사(Linking Verb)로 구분합니다. 불완전 자동사를 영어로는 linking verb라고 부르는데, 주어와 그 뒤의 형용사/명사를 연결해주는 동사입니다. 대표적인 불완전 자동사는 be동사이죠.

---

1. **완전 자동사(Verb Intransitive)**
   〈주어 + 동사〉 형태의 문장에서 쓰이며, '부사' 및 '전치사를 동반한 부사구'가 함께 쓰이는 경우가 많죠.

   The servant left the next day.
   　주어　　　동사 시간을 나타내는 부사구

2. **불완전 자동사(Linking Verb)**
   〈주어 + 동사 + 형용사/명사〉 형태의 문장으로 쓰여 '~는 ~이다'는 의미를 나타냅니다. 이때 동사 뒤에 오는 형용사/명사는 일반적으로 주어를 보충설명해 주므로 '보어'라 불리죠.

   My parents were old.
   　주어　　be동사　형용사(보어): My parents를 보충설명

   Rebekah was a sister of Laban.
   　주어　　be동사　명사(보어): Rebekah를 보충설명

3. **be동사가 때로는 완전 자동사로 쓰이는 경우도 있습니다.**
   〈주어 + be동사 + 장소 부사구〉는 '~가 …에 있다'는 의미로 이때 be동사는 완전 자동사랍니다.

   They were in the field.
   　주어　be동사 장소를 나타내는 부사구

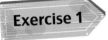
Exercise 1

다음은 모두 be동사가 쓰인 문장으로, 밑줄 친 부분은 be동사와 밀접한 관계가 있습니다. 밑줄 친 부분이 문법적으로 어떤 역할을 하는지 써보세요.
　　　　　　　　　　　　　　　예 명사(noun), 형용사(adjective), 장소(location)

1 We are <u>Christians</u>.

2 "Abraham! Abraham!" "<u>Here</u> I am."

3 He is <u>hungry</u>.

4 They are <u>upstairs</u>.

5 Cats are <u>animals</u>.

Exercise 2 이제 be동사를 이용하여 간단한 문장을 만들어 볼까요?

---

1 우리는 집에 있다. (at home)

~~~~~~
~~~~~~~~~~~~~~~~~~~~~~~ .

---

2 진희는 똑똑하다. (smart)

~~~~~~ .

---

3 민수와 진희는 학생이다.

~~~~~~
~~~~~~~~~~~~~~~~~~~~~~~ .

A   Let's Memorize the Patterns! 05-5

동사 believe(믿다)는 전치사 in을 함께 쓰느냐, 아니냐에 따라 그 의미가 약간 달라질 수 있습니다.

- believe somebody/something ~가 한 말/~이 진실임을 믿다
- believe that 주어 + 동사 ~가 …임을 믿다
- believe in somebody ~의 능력을 믿다[신뢰한다]
- believe in something ~의 존재를 믿다

I don't **believe** you.

난 네가 한 말을 믿지 않아. (한 말이 사실인 것에 대한 믿음)

I **believe in** you.

난 너의 능력을 믿어. (능력에 대한 믿음)

I **believe that** you're right.

난 네가 옳다고 믿어. (네가 옳다는 사실에 대한 믿음)

I **believe in** God.

난 하나님을 믿어. (하나님의 존재에 대한 믿음)

B   Let's Talk: Pair Work

두 명씩 한 조를 만들어 보세요. 그런 후 다음에 제시된 문장을 사용하여 서로 영어로 대화해 보세요.

1	Partner A	I can't wake up in the morning without Mom's help.
	Partner B	Believe in yourself that you can do it.
	Partner A	_____.
	Partner B	Believe in yourself that _____.
2	Partner A	Do you believe that _____.
	Partner B	Sure. (동의하는 경우) / No, I don't think so. (동의하지 않는 경우)

A My Confession 05-6

After Isaac moved into Egypt, he dug four wells. Even though he succeeded in digging the first two wells, he gave them up for the Philistine shepherds because he did not want to quarrel with them. These generous actions allowed Isaac and his shepherds to water their flocks from the last two wells without being bothered by the Philistines. Why did Isaac give the first two wells to the Philistines? Was he afraid of the Philistines? Or did he believe God always walked with him and would give him whatever he wanted? Do you also believe that God is always with you even in difficulties? Share your idea with group members and write down your idea in English if possible.

이삭은 애굽으로 거처를 옮긴 뒤 우물 네 개를 팠습니다. 처음 두 개의 우물을 파는 데 성공했지만, 블레셋 사람들과 다투고 싶지 않았기 때문에 처음 두 우물을 블레셋 사람들에게 양보해 주었습니다. 이 관대한 행동 때문에 이삭과 목자들은 블레셋 사람들과 불화를 일으키지 않고 나머지 두 우물에서 가축들에게 물을 먹일 수 있었습니다. 왜 이삭이 처음 두 개의 우물을 블레셋 사람들에게 주었을까요? 블레셋 사람들이 두려웠을까요? 아니면 하나님께서 항상 그와 함께하고 그가 원하는 것이라면 무엇이든 주신다는 것을 믿었기 때문일까요? 여러분 또한 어려움 속에서도 하나님께서 함께하심을 믿나요? 다른 친구들과 이야기를 나누어 본 후 여러분의 생각을 가능하면 영어로 써보세요.

 영어로 쓰기가 힘들다면 우리말로 써도 괜찮습니다.

B Let's Pray! 🎧 05-7

오늘은 아침 기도를 영어로 써볼까요? 하루를 하나님의 보살핌 아래 잘 지낼 수 있기를 바라는 한 어린이의 기도입니다.

Now I raise me up from sleep.

I thank the Lord who did me keep.

All through the night; and to Him pray

That He may keep me through the day.

All which for Jesus's sake, I say.

Amen.

이제 막 잠자리에서 일어났습니다.
밤새 저를 지켜주신 하나님께 감사드립니다.
낮에도 저를 지켜주시기를 기도합니다.
예수님의 이름으로 이 모든 기도를 드립니다.
아멘.

Write a Prayer for Yourself!

이제 여러분만의 아침 기도를 해볼까요? 위의 예처럼 간단하게 영어로 기도를 써보세요.

Dear Lord,

Amen.

Abraham and Isaac

(to the tune 'Dance to Your Daddy')

Abraham was tested, oh so sorely tested.
He'd just got a message, from the living God.
"Go down to Moriah, sacrifice your boy there!
Burn him as an offering, then report to me!"

Early the next morning, as the day was dawning,
saddled up his donkey, set off on his way.
Isaac travelled with him, trusting and unknowing.
'Lamb for the burnt offering,' Abraham looked grim.

"Come to your daddy, my little laddie,
don't think badly of me, I've a job to do!

He put him on an altar, and he didn't falter.
Raised his knife to slay him, then he heard a voice!

"Abraham don't hurt him, lay no hand upon him!
Now God knows you're faithful, offered him your son."

Now what takes the biscuit, from a nearby thicket,
Ab'ram found a ram there, offered it instead!

"Dance to your daddy, my little laddie,
God has saved us both now
I am dancing too!"

(instrumental & repeat last chorus)

used with permission www.sheilahamil.co.uk

06

Father of the Twelve Tribes of Israel

All these are the twelve tribes of Israel, and this is what their father said to

them when he blessed them giving each the blessing appropriate to him.

(Gen. 49:28) 📖

Who Am I?

STEP 1 Listen!

오디오를 듣고 말하고 있는 인물이 누구인지 알아맞혀 보세요.

A

🎧 06-1

Who am I?

✏

B

🎧 06-2

✏

Who am I?

Script

A | I was a twin. I had a dream about a ladder with the top reaching heaven. In my dream God told me that my offspring and I would be given the land before me. Because My mother and I tricked Father into giving me the blessing meant for my elder brother, I was sent to my uncle, Laban's home. Laban tricked me into getting married to Leah instead of Rachel after the first seven years of work. I had to work for another seven years in order to get married to Rachel. At Panel, my name was changed to "Israel" after I wrestled with God in the form of a man. I was the father of the twelve tribes of Israel. Who am I?

B | I was a twin. Some people say my name means 'hairy' or 'red' as I was described in the Bible, but it is not certain. I was the firstborn in my family. I was my father's favorite son. But I sold my birthright to my younger brother for a meal of lentil stew and bread. My father was tricked into giving Jacob the blessings meant for me by Mother and my younger brother. I was very angry when I realized that my blessings from Father were stolen. But I forgave my younger brother when he offered his olive branch, giving me presents. Who am I?

STEP 2 Speak!

오디오를 듣고 큰소리로 따라 읽어 보세요.

  06-3

 ### Jacob: Father of the Twelve Tribes[1] of Israel

He was a twin.

He had a dream about a ladder[2] with the top reaching heaven.

In his dream God told him that he and his offspring[3] would be given the land before him. (Gen. 28: 12-15)

He and his mother tricked Isaac into giving him the blessing meant for Esau, so he was sent to his Uncle Laban's home.

He was tricked by Laban into getting married to Leah instead of[4] Rachel after the first seven years of work.

He had to work another seven years in order to get married to Rachel.

At Panel, his name was changed to "Israel" after he wrestled[5] with God in the form of a man. (Gen. 32: 24-30) He was the father of the twelve tribes of Israel.

Words and Idioms   Consult the index dictionary if needed.

1 tribe: a large group of related families who live in the same area and share a common language, religion, and customs 부족

2 ladder:

3 offspring:

4 instead of:

5 wrestle:

 06-4

 Esau: The Elder Brother of Jacob

He was a twin.

Some people say that Esau means 'hairy' or 'red' as he was described in the Bible (Gen. 25:25), but it is not certain.

He was the firstborn in that family.

He was Isaac's favorite son.

He sold his birthright[1] to his younger brother for a meal of lentil[2] stew[3] and bread.

His father was tricked into giving Jacob the blessings meant for him by Rebekah and Jacob.

He was very angry when he realized that Isaac's blessings were stolen.

He forgave Jacob when Jacob offered his olive branch,[4] giving presents.[5]

| Words and Idioms | Consult the index dictionary if needed.

1 birthright: a right, privilege, or possession to which a person is entitled by birth 장자상속권

2 lentil:

3 stew:

4 offer one's olive branch:

5 present:

동사의 종류 (Verbs 3): 수여동사

동사 give는 일반적으로 수여동사라 불리며, give 동사 다음에 '사람(somebody)'과 '사물(something)' 중 어떤 것이 오느냐에 따라 전치사 to가 들어가기도 합니다.

---

1. **give** + somebody + something ~을 …에게 주다

   Isaac gave Jacob the blessing meant for Esau.
   　　　　　사람(야곱에게)　 에서에게 주려 했던 축복을

2. **give** + something + **to** somebody ~에게 …을 주다

   Isaac gave the blessings to Jacob.
   　　　　　축복을(something) 야곱에게(to somebody)

3. **give** + 대명사의 목적격(it, them) + **to** somebody 대명사(it, them)의 목적격을 ~에게 주다

   이 경우 순서는 불변입니다.

   Isaac **gave** them **to** Jacob.
   　　　　　　대명사　 to 사람 (순서 불변)

동사 give와 같은 종류의 동사로는 다음과 같은 것들이 있습니다.

send 보내다　**show** 보여주다　**lend** 빌려주다　**pass** 전해주다, 건네주다

Mom **sent** me a letter. = Mom **sent** a letter **to** me. 엄마는 내게 편지를 보내셨다.

★ a letter 대신 it을 쓸 경우: Mom sent it to me.

Jinsu **showed** me his field trip pictures.

= Jinsu **showed** his field trip pictures **to** me. 진수는 내게 현장학습 사진을 보여주었다.

★ his field trip pictures 대신 them을 쓸 경우: Jinsu showed them to me.

I will **lend** Minhee some money. = I will **lend** some money **to** Minhee.

난 민희에게 돈을 좀 빌려줄 것이다.

1	그거 내 핸드폰(cell phone)이야. 나한 테 줄래?	That's my _____ . Can you _____ ?
2	나는 내 학생증(student ID card)을 선생님에게 보여드렸다.	I _____ .
3	소금 좀 건네주시겠어요?	Could you _____ ?
4	이력서(resume)는 메일로(by email) 저희에게 보내주시면 됩니다.	You can _____ .
5	네 노트북(laptop) 좀 빌려줄 수 있 어?	Can you _____ ?

A Let's Memorize the Patterns! 06-5

- another 또 다른, 또 하나
  ▶ 앞에서 나온 명사와 같은 종류로 '하나 더'를 의미합니다. 〈an + other〉가 합한 것이므로 꼭 단수 명사만을 써야 한다는 것은 기본 상식이죠. 단, '시간, 돈, 거리'의 경우에는 another 다음에 복수형을 쓰기도 한다는 점을 추가 상식으로 알아두세요.

- the other 다른 하나
  ▶ 앞에서 말한 명사 두 개 중에서 '남은 하나'를 가리킵니다. 여러 개의 명사 중에서 한 개를 언급하고 '남은 것들'을 가리킬 때는 복수형(the others)으로 써야 하죠.

Can I have **another** serving of soup? 국 한 그릇 더 먹어도 되나요?
▶ 이미 한 그릇의 국을 먹었기 때문에 똑같은 종류의 국을 더 주문하는 경우입니다.

Jacob had to work **another** seven years in order to get married to Rachel.
야곱은 라헬과 결혼하기 위해 또 7년을 더 일해야 했어요.
▶ 라헬과 결혼하기 위해 7년을 일했지만 대신 언니 레아와 결혼하고, 이후 똑같은 종류의 일을 7년 더 한 것이므로 another를 쓴 거죠.

I have two oranges. I'm going to eat **one**. Do you want to eat **the other**?
오렌지가 두 개 있어요. 하나 먹으려고 하는데 다른 하나 드시겠어요?

There are four students in my class. **One** is from Seoul. **The others** are from Ilsan.
내 수업에 학생이 네 명 있어요. 한 명은 서울 출신인데 다른 학생들은 일산에서 왔어요.

B Let's Talk: Pair Work

두 명씩 한 조를 만들어 보세요. 그런 후 다음에 제시된 문장을 사용하여 서로 영어로 대화해 보세요.

1	Partner A	Thanks for the _____. It's delicious.
		(cookies, candies, chocolates 등 원하는 맛있는 것을 넣어보세요.)
	Partner B	There are plenty more. Do you want another?
2	Partner A	How many languages can you speak?
	Partner B	Two. One is _____ and the other is _____.

77

A My Confession 06-6

Some people say that Jacob is a trickster because he earned Esau's birthright and Isaac's blessings by tricks. But from our points of view, he can be a brave and energetic man who has tried to overcome his weaknesses. As a second-born child, he could not have got the birthright and the blessings from his father. He could earn them through his efforts. He could also be very scared when he decided to go and ask forgiveness from his elder brother, Esau. But he chose to do it and reconciled with his brother. Do you also agree with the idea that Jacob is a trickster? Share your idea with group members and write down your idea in English if possible.

야곱이 에서의 장자권과 이삭의 축복을 속임수로 얻었기 때문에 야곱을 책략꾼이라 부르는 사람들도 있습니다. 그러나 현대적 관점에서 볼 때 그는 자신의 약점을 이겨내려고 한 용감하고 열정적인 사람일 수도 있습니다. 둘째 아들로서 그는 장자권과 아버지의 축복을 얻을 수 없었습니다. 그는 자신의 노력으로 이런 것들을 얻을 수 있었죠. 그는 또한 형, 에서에게 가서 용서를 빌려고 결심했을 때 매우 겁이 났을 수도 있었습니다. 그러나 그는 그렇게 하기로 선택했고 형과 화해를 했습니다. 여러분도 야곱이 책략꾼이라는 의견에 동의하나요? 다른 친구들과 이야기를 나누어 본 후 여러분의 생각을 가능하다면 영어로 써보세요.

 영어로 쓰기가 힘들다면 우리말로 써도 괜찮습니다.

 **B** **Let's Pray!** 🎧 06-7

다음은 야곱이 길을 떠나며 하나님께 드린 기도를 우리가 알기 쉽도록 변형한 것입니다. 우리도 여행을 떠날 기회가 있습니다. 이럴 때 야곱의 기도를 생각해보고 우리의 기도를 영어로 드려봅시다.

Dear Lord,

Show me that you are always with me.

Take care of me on my journey.

Make sure that I have food and everything I need.

Most of all, bring me safely home.

> 사랑의 주님,
> 저와 항상 함께 해주시고,
> 여행 중에 저를 돌봐주소서.
> 일용할 양식과 필요한 것을 주시고,
> 무엇보다도 무사히 집으로 인도해 주소서.

 Write a Prayer for Yourself!

이제 여러분의 여행 기도를 써볼까요? 위의 예처럼 간단하게 영어로 기도를 써보세요.

Dear Lord,

Amen.

Jacob's Dream

*(to the tunes 'Swing Low, Sweet Chariot' 'When the Saints Go Marching In'
and 'I'm Gonna Sing, Sing, Sing')*

So Jacob journeyed on,
and when it was time for bed,
taking a stone, he made a pillow
and placed it under his head.

'Twas there he dreamed a dream,
oh such a dream, of a stairway, so immense.
From the earth it reached up high,
he was sure it touched the sky.
"What a night! What a dream!" Jacob sighed.

There were angels going up,
there were angels coming down,
on that stairway oh so high.
As he slept there on the ground,
this is what he found,
God spoke, there above him, right out loud.

*"I am the Lord your God, of Isaac and
Abraham.
To you and all of your descendants,
I'm giving you this land.
And they will bless the world,
like dust they'll spread out far.
And I'll be with you all your days,
watch you wherever you are!"*

"Surely God is in this place!
Surely God is in this place!

He was here and I knew it not!
House of God, heaven's gate.
How awesome is this place,
it must never be forgot."
*(now sing this last verse again along with the
next two, all three together)*

"This is the house of God. *(Swing low tune)*
He was here and I knew it not!
Surely this is the gate of heaven, it must
never be forgot!"

"House of God! Heaven's gate! *(When the
saints)*
God was here I knew it not!
Oh how very awesome is this place,
it must never be forgot."
(repeat this last verse at the end)

07

The Dreamer and Dream Interpreter

Pharaoh said to Joseph, "I had a dream, and no one can interpret it. But I have heard it said of you that when you hear a dream you can interpret it." "I cannot do it," Joseph replied to Pharaoh, "but God will give Pharaoh the answer he desires."

(Gen. 41:15-16) 📖

STEP 1 Listen!

오디오를 듣고 말하고 있는 인물이 누구인지 알아맞혀 보세요.

A

🎧 07-1

✏️

Who am I?

B

🎧 07-2

✏️

Who am I?

A | I was my father's favorite son, so he gave me a coat with long sleeves. At 17 I had two figurative dreams. In my first dream, my brothers were bowing to me. In my second dream, my father and mother bowed to me also. I told these two dreams to my brothers and this made my brothers angry. I was sold and taken to Egypt. In prison, my good ability to interpret dreams could be proved, so I was called to interpret Pharaoh's dreams. After that, I rose to power and helped save Egypt from starvation during a long famine. I had all of my family move to Egypt and we lived there for many years. Who am I?

B | I was Joseph's oldest brother. My mother's name was Leah, the first daughter of Laban. My father said to me, "You are my firstborn, my might, the first sign of my strength, excelling in honor, excelling in power," (Gen. 49:3) but his favorite son was always Joseph. I prevented my younger brothers from killing Joseph. I also planned to save his life from my younger brothers, but they sold him when I was not with them. I had always felt guilty about it before I met Joseph in Egypt. My family and descendants lived in Egypt for many years. I became the father of one of the twelve tribes of Israel. Who am I?

STEP 2 Speak!

오디오를 듣고 큰소리로 따라 읽어 보세요.

  07-3

 ## Joseph: The Dreamer and Dream Interpreter

Joseph was Isaac's favorite son, so Isaac gave him a coat with long sleeves.

He had two figurative[1] dreams when he was seventeen.

In his first dream, his brothers were bowing[2] to him.

In his second dream, his father and mother bowed to him also.

He told these two dreams to his brothers and this made them angry.

He was sold and taken to Egypt.

In prison, his good ability to interpret[3] dreams could be proved,[4] so he was called to interpret Pharaoh's dreams.

After that, he rose to power and helped save Egypt from starvation[5] during a long famine.

He had all of his family move to Egypt and they lived there for many years.

> **Words and Idioms** Consult the index dictionary if needed.

1 figurative: using words not in their normal literal meaning but in a way that makes a description more interesting or impressive 비유적인

2 bow:

3 interpret:

4 prove:

5 starvation:

83

07-4

 Reuben: Joseph's oldest brother

Reuben was Joseph's oldest brother.

His mother's name was Leah, the first daughter of Laban.

His father said to me, "You are my firstborn, my might, the first sign[1] of my strength,

excelling[2] in honor, excelling in power." (Gen. 49:3)

But Father's favorite son was always Joseph.

He prevented[3] his younger brothers from killing Joseph.

He also planned to save Joseph's life from his brothers, but they sold him when Reuben

was not with them.

He had always felt guilty[4] about it before he met Joseph in Egypt.

His family and descendants[5] lived in Egypt for many years.

He became the father of one of the twelve tribes[6] of Israel.

Words and Idioms | Consult the index dictionary if needed.

1 sign: a piece of evidence that something is happening or that something exists 징조

2 excel:

3 prevent:

4 guilty:

5 descendant:

6 tribe:

동사의 종류 (Verbs 4): 사역동사

• have + somebody + 동사원형 ~가 …하게 하다
동사 have가 '가지다'의 뜻이 아니라 '~가 …하게 하다'라는 뜻을 가질 때 이를 '사역동사 (Causative Verb)' 라 부릅니다.
have와 같은 역할을 하는 '사역동사'에는 make, let 등도 있습니다.

다음의 두 문장은 우리말로 모두 '엄마는 아빠에게 전구를 갈게 하셨다.'입니다. 하지만 그 의미는 약간 차이가 있죠. 어떻게 차이가 날까요?

Mom had Dad <u>change</u> the light bulb.
Mom made Dad <u>change</u> the light bulb.

1 가장 큰 차이는 '어떻게' 시켰는지의 정도입니다. 사역동사 have의 경우는 '요청하는(request)' 경우 입니다. '엄마는 아빠에게 전구를 갈아달라'고 요청한 것이죠. 그래서 아빠가 전구를 간 것입니다.

2 make의 경우는 '하기 싫은데 억지로 시킨' 것입니다. 두 번째 문장의 경우 아빠는 그냥 누워 쉬고 싶은데(?) 엄마의 강권으로 전구를 간 것이죠.

3 마지막으로 사역동사 let은 '~가 원하는 것을 허락해서 하게 하는 경우'를 뜻합니다.

Please let me <u>go</u>. 제발 가게 해 주세요.

내가 가기를 원하니까 갈 수 있도록 상대방의 허락을 구하는 것이라 할 수 있죠.

이제 사역동사 have, make, let의 차이를 각각 한 줄로 정리해 볼까요?

---

1. **have + somebody + 동사원형** ~에게 …하라고 요청해 하게 하다

2. **make + somebody + 동사원형** ~에게 …을 억지로 시키다 (하지 않으면 안 되게 하다)

3. **let + somebody + 동사원형** ~에게 …을 하는 것을 허락해서 하게 하다

 **Exercise** have, make, let 중에서 어떤 동사를 써야 할지 생각하면서 다음 문장을 영작해 보세요.

1	엄마는 저녁 먹기 전에 내게 손을 씻게 하셨다. (나는 귀찮아서 하기 싫었는데 억지로)	Mom _____ me _____ _____ before dinner.
2	민주가 네게 전화하도록 할게.	I'll _____ Minju _____.
3	제 소개를 하게 해주세요.	_____ _____ .

A Let's Memorize the Patterns! 07-5

- 주어 + help + 사람 + (to) 동사원형 ~가 …하는 것을 돕다
  ▶ '사람'이 '동사원형'의 일을 하는 것을 돕는다는 뜻으로, '사람'이 일을 하는 주체이고, '주어'는 그 일을 돕는 역할을 하는 것을 나타냅니다.

- 주어 + help + (to) 동사원형 ~를 하는 것을 돕다
  ▶ '동사원형'을 하는 사람이 나와 있지 않은 경우로, '주어'가 주체입니다.

Moses **helped** Pharaoh save Egypt from starvation during a long famine.
▶ 바로가 오랜 기간 굶주린 애굽을 구하는 일을 모세가 돕는 것
▶ 바로가 주체이고 모세가 돕는 역할

Moses **helped** save Egypt from starvation during a long famine.
▶ 모세가 주체가 되어 오랜 기간 굶주린 애굽을 돕는 것

Can you **help** me do dishes?
설거지하는 거 좀 도와줄래?

Fifteen minutes' nap will **help** recharge our batteries.
15분간 낮잠을 자면 우린 재충전이 될 거야.

B ## Let's Talk: Pair Work

도와달라고 말하고 싶을 때	도움에 감사할 때
Help!	Thanks for your help.
I need help!	Thanks for helping me out.
I need some help.	▶ help out은 주로 말할 때 쓰입니다.
Can you help me, please?	I really appreciate your help.
Will you help me?	▶ 매우 정중한 표현입니다.
I would like your help.	

위의 표현들을 사용하여 대화를 해볼까요? 두 명씩 한 조를 만들어 보세요. 그런 후 다음에 제시된 문장을 사용하여 서로 영어로 대화해 보세요.

Partner A Will you help me?

Partner B Sure. How can I help you?

Partner A Can you tell me how to get to the library?

Partner B _____.

Partner A Thanks for helping me out.

A　My Confession 07-6

Joseph always believed that God was with him even when he was sold to Egypt and sent into prison. Because of this strong belief, Joseph, the second-in-command over Egypt, could say to his brothers, "It was not you who sent me here, but God. He made me father to Pharaoh, lord of his entire household and ruler of all Egypt." (Gen. 45:8) If Joseph had not had this strong faith, what kind of things could have happened to him? Could he survive in Egypt and become the second-in-command over Egypt? Moreover, could he forgive his brothers who sold himself to Egypt? Share your idea with group members and write down your idea in English if possible.

요셉은 자신이 애굽에 팔려가고, 감옥에 갇혀 있을 때조차도 하나님께서 자신과 함께 하심을 믿었습니다. 이런 강한 믿음 때문에 애굽의 제2인자로서 요셉은 형제들에게 "그런즉 나를 이리로 보낸 이는 당신들이 아니요, 하나님이시라. 하나님이 나를 바로에게 아버지로 삼으시고 그 온 집의 주로 삼으시며 애굽 온 땅의 통치자로 삼으셨나이다."라고 말할 수 있었죠.(창세기 45:8) 요셉이 이처럼 강한 믿음을 가지지 않았다면 어떤 일이 그에게 일어날 수 있었을까요? 그는 애굽에서 살아남아 애굽의 제2인자가 될 수 있었을까요? 더욱이 애굽으로 자신을 팔아버린 형제들을 용서할 수 있었을까요? 다른 친구들과 이야기를 나누어 본 후 여러분의 생각을 가능하면 영어로 써보세요.

 영어로 쓰기가 힘들다면 우리말로 써도 괜찮습니다.

 **Let's Pray!** 🎧 07-7

다음은 영국의 유명한 시인인 John Donne(1573–1631)이 쓴 기도입니다. 시간이 있을 때마다 이 기도문을 외우며 하나님께서 우리와 함께하지 않으면 결코 안 된다는 걸 꼭 기억하세요.

O Lord, never suffer us to think that we can stand by ourselves, and not need thee.

> 오 하나님. 우리가 혼자 힘으로 설 수 있고 당신을 필요로 하지 않는다고 생각하는 수고를 하지 않게 해주세요.

 Write a Prayer for Yourself!

오늘의 기도를 간단하게 영어로 써보세요.

Dear Lord,

Amen.

A Poem & Song

Joseph's Brothers
(verses to the tune 'Horsey Horsey')

Joseph's brothers they were grim;
sent him off to Egypt 'cos they didn't like him.
But God had a plan ~ a very great plan,
to save him and his family.

Why you might ask did his brothers hate him?
Why just walk away and not save him?
The reason why was jealousy.
He was daddy's favourite, the bee's knees!
Not only that, he'd been having dreams.
Dreams of greatness so it seems.
And that is the reason why they hated him,
that is the reason I say 'grim'.

So off he went and he served God well.
It wasn't very nice in a prison cell,
But God had a plan ~ a very great plan,
to save him and his family.

Why you might ask was he there in jail?
Why should a good boy like him fail?
False accusations put him there,
false they were and it wasn't fair!
But inside prison his gifts he practised,
Interpretin' dreams of those who asked him.
But even though he served God well,
he spent more years in that prison cell!

Now we go to the other extreme,
he helped Pharaoh with his dreams,
and God had a plan ~ a very great plan,
to save him and his family.

So how come Joseph got to be free?
A butler spoke for him you see.
Pharaoh was having these dreams so vile,
lean cows, fat cows by the Nile;
of healthy corn eaten up by withered.
All these dreams made Pharaoh shiver,
all of these dreams Joseph examined,
Said, "King, there's gonna be a famine!"

Pharaoh was grateful, by and large.
Then and there, put him in charge,
for God had a plan ~ a very great plan,
to save him and his family.

Then his brothers came on by, they were hungry and their mouths were dry. But Joseph didn't blame them, and he told them how, God had saved their family.

used with permission www.sheilahamil.co.uk

Joseph was given authority,
Pharaoh was the only one greater than he!
He stored up grain just as expected,
people bowed before him, he was so respected.
Storehouses sprang up everywhere,
before the land turned dry and bare!
Seven years of plenty, then seven years of famine.
But Joseph stayed on top of all the admin.

Then came the famine and it wasn't good
But Joseph stored up lots of food.
See God had a plan ~ a very great plan,
to save him and his family.

What you might ask did his family do,
When the famine hit his homeland too?
Like many families way out there
they were hungry, caught out in despair.
The starving, the desperate to Egypt came.
Joseph's plans brought the city fame.
For all travelled there to beg for their grain,
from the only man around who could actually save them.

Then his brothers came on by.
They were hungry and their mouths were dry.
But Joseph didn't blame them, and he told them how God had saved their family.

His older brothers before him came,
begging for food, so Joseph played a game.
Called them spies, used tricks to upset them.
Wouldn't you done it, just to get back at them?
To cut a story short, when he told them who he was,
you could have heard a pin drop; that's because they recalled their terrible deed.
But when Joseph forgave them,
they were so relieved!

You see God had a plan to save him and his family.

08

The Great Liberator of the Israelites

Now the LORD spoke to Moses and Aaron about the Israelites and

Pharaoh king of Egypt, and He commanded them to bring the Israelites

out of Egypt. (Exod. 6:13) 📖

STEP 1 Listen!

오디오를 듣고 말하고 있는 인물이 누구인지 알아맞혀 보세요.

A

🎧 08-1

Who am I? ✏️

B

🎧 08-2

✏️

Who am I?

Script

A | I was born in Egypt. My mother hid me in the basket among the reeds. I was discovered and raised by Pharaoh's daughter. I killed an Egyptian who was beating an Israelite, interfered with a quarrel between two Hebrews, and fled to Midian. I heard God calling me from a burning bush. I protested, but finally agreed to go when God sent my brother Aaron, with me. As a result of ten plagues brought on Egypt, I took the Israelites out of Egypt. On Mount Sinai, I was given the Ten Commandments and the conquest of Canaan was promised by God. I led the Israelites out of Egypt, but I could not enter the Promised Land. I died at 120 years of age and was buried in Moab. Who am I?

B | I was an elder brother of Moses. I had a sister called Miriam. She was famous as a smart girl who watched over baby Moses in a basket among the reeds. Moses was a poor speaker, so God promised him to send me as his prophet. It was me who told Pharaoh, "Let the Israelites go." My staff was thrown down in front of Pharaoh and became a snake. I regret helping the people of Israel build a golden calf. This act of disobedience ended in God's bringing a plague on the Israelites. I was the first priest of Israel. Like my brother and sister, I could not enter the Promised Land. Who am I?

오디오를 듣고 큰소리로 따라 읽어 보세요.

  08-3

 Moses: The Great Liberator

Moses was born in Egypt.

His mother hid Moses in the basket[1] among the reeds.[2]

He was discovered[3] and raised by Pharaoh's daughter.

He killed an Egyptian who was beating an Israelite, interfered[4] with a quarrel between two Hebrews, and fled to Midian.

He heard God calling him from a burning bush.

He protested,[5] but finally agreed to go when God sent his brother Aaron, with him.

He took the Israelites out of Egypt as a result of[6] ten plagues[7] brought on Egypt.

On Mount Sinai, he was given the Ten Commandments and the conquest[8] of Canaan was promised by God.

He led the Israelites out of Egypt, but he could not enter the Promised Land.

He died at 120 years of age and was buried[9] in Moab.

1 basket: a container for carrying or keeping things in 바구니

2 reed:

3 discover:

4 interfere:

5 protest:

6 as a result of:

7 plague:

8 conquest:

9 bury:

08-4

 Aaron: The First Priest of Israel

Aaron was an elder brother of Moses.

He had a sister called Miriam. She was famous as a smart girl who was watching over baby Moses in a basket among the reeds.

Aaron was sent as Moses' prophet[1] by God because Moses was a poor speaker.

He told Pharaoh, "Let the Israelites go."

His staff[2] was thrown down in front of Pharaoh and became a snake.

He helped the people of Israel build a golden calf,[3] and this act of disobedience[4] ended in God's bringing a plague on the Israelites.

He was the first priest[5] of Israel.

Like his brother and sister, he could not enter the Promised Land.

Words and Idioms ┆ Consult the index dictionary if needed.

1 prophet: a person who is believed to be chosen by God to say the things that God wants to tell people 예언자, 사제

2 staff:

3 calf:

4 disobedience:

5 priest:

동사의 종류 (Verbs 5): 지각동사

동사 hear(듣다)는 '지각동사'라 불립니다. 이 지각동사는 '~가 …하는 것을 듣다'라는 문장 유형을 가질. 때 다음과 같이 사용되죠.

---

1. 주어 + hear + somebody + **동사원형** ~가 …하는 것을 듣다

2. 주어 + hear + somebody + -ing ~가 …하고 있는 것을 듣다 (하고 있는 것을 강조하고 싶을 때)

---

hear와 동일한 문장 형태를 지니는 동사들에는 다음과 같은 것들이 있습니다.

see 보다   **watch** 지켜보다   **smell** 냄새를 맡다

Moses **heard** God calling him from a burning bush.
모세는 하나님이 불타는 떨기나무에서 자신을 부르는 소리를 들었다.

I **saw** him walking to me. 나는 그가 내게 걸어오는 것을 보았다.

Dad is busy. He can't **hear** the phone ring (ringing).
아빠는 바쁘시다. 아빠는 전화벨이 울리는 소리를 못 들으신다.

Do you **smell** something burning? 뭔가 타는 냄새가 나지?

 **Exercise** 괄호 안의 우리말을 보고 다음 빈칸에 적합한 단어를 넣으세요.

---

1   I _____ Mom _____ me from the basement. (듣다 / 부르다)

---

2   We can _____ the people _____ in the City Hall. (보다 / 모이다)

---

3   I don't want to _____ Mom _____ my younger brother. (보다 / 야단치다)

---

4   Can you _____ the beef stew _____? (냄새나다 / 타다)

A Let's Memorize the Patterns! 08-5

'가난한'이란 대표적 의미로 잘 알려진 poor는 능력에 관계되어 쓰일 경우, '잘 못하는'이란 의미가 됩니다.

- 주어 + be동사 + (a) poor 명사 ~을 잘 못하다
- 주어 + be동사 + poor at/in 명사 ~을 잘 못하다

poor의 반대는 good(잘하는)입니다. 아래 예문들에 모두 poor 대신 good을 넣어서도 말해보세요.

Moses was a poor speaker.
모세는 말을 잘 못합니다.

They are poor talkers.
저들은 말을 잘 못해. ▶ 주어 They가 복수이므로 보어 자리에 오는 명사도 복수형(talkers)으로 써야 합니다.

I am poor at math.
난 수학을 잘 못해.

They are poor at English.
저 사람들은 영어를 잘 못해. ▶ 주어 they가 복수형이라도 전치사 at 다음에 복수형 명사를 쓰지 않습니다.

My grandmother is poor in health.
저희 할머니는 건강이 안 좋으세요.

B Let's Talk: Pair Work

두 명씩 한 조를 만들어 보세요. 그런 후 다음에 제시된 문장을 사용하여 서로 영어로 대화해 보세요.

1	Partner A	I'm poor at _(English)_ .
	Partner B	I don't think so. _(Your English)_ is good.
2	Partner A	She's _(a good speaker)_ !
	Partner B	_(Her speech about eco schools)_ was really good.

A My Confession 🎧 08-6

When God told Moses to go to Pharaoh and say to him, "Let My people go!", Moses protested, asking three questions of God. The first one was "Who am I that I should lead the Israelites out of Egypt?" (Exod. 3:11) The second one was "Who shall I tell them sent me?" (Exod. 3:13) The third one was "What if they do not believe me? What if they will not listen?" (Exod. 4:1) Even though God gave all the answers to these three questions, Moses still protested, speaking to God, "O Lord, I don't speak very well, and my speech is slow." (Exod. 4:10) "Please send someone else." (Exod. 4:13) In spite of his protests, Moses was sent to Egypt. What do you think made Moses leave for Egypt? If God asks you to do something, what kinds of attitudes are needed? Share your idea with group members and write down your idea in English if you can.

하나님께서 모세를 바로에게 보내어 "내 백성을 가게 하라"고 말씀하셨을 때, 모세는 세 가지 질문을 하나님께 하면서 이의를 제기했습니다. 첫 번째 질문은 "내가 누구이기에 이스라엘 자손을 애굽에서 인도하여 내리이까?"였습니다.(출애굽기 3:11) 두 번째 질문은 "그들에게 누가 나를 보냈다고 말하리이까?"였습니다.(출애굽기 3:13) 세 번째 질문은 "그들이 나를 믿지 아니하며 내 말을 듣지 아니하면 어찌하리까?"였습니다.(출애굽기 4:1) 하나님께서는 이 세 가지 질문에 모두 답하셨지만 모세는 여전히 말을 듣지 않았습니다. 모세는 하나님께 아뢰었습니다. "오 주여, 나는 본래 말을 잘하지 못하는 자이며, 그래서 연설은 어눌하나이다."(출애굽기 4:10) "다른 자를 보내소서."(출애굽기 4:13) 하나님의 명령을 피하려는 노력에도 불구하고 모세는 애굽을 향해 떠나게 되었습니다. 모세가 이렇게 애굽으로 떠나게 된 이유가 여러분은 무엇이라 생각하나요? 만약 하나님께서 무언가를 하라고 명령하시면 어떤 태도를 가져야 할까요? 다른 친구들과 이야기를 나누어 본 후 여러분의 생각을 가능하면 영어로 써보세요.

먼저 모세의 질문에 적합한 하나님의 답을 아래에서 찾아보세요.

God's answers

(1) Your brother Aaron speaks very well. He will go with you. Tell him what to say and he will say it.

(2) I AM that I AM. Tell them I AM sent you.

(3) "If they do not believe you, take some water from the Nile River and pour it on the ground. It will become blood."

(4) I will be with you.

여러분의 생각을 써보세요. 영어로 쓰기가 힘들다면 우리말로 써도 괜찮습니다.

B Let's Memorize the Ten Commandments! 08-7

God spoke all these words, ten commandments. Here is what God says:

1. You shall have no other gods but Me.

2. Do not treat anything else as God.

3. You shall not use the name of the Lord to swear[1] or curse.[2]

4. You shall keep the Sabbath Day[3] holy.

5. Honour your father and your mother.

6. You shall not commit murder.

7. You shall not commit adultery.[4]

8. You shall not steal.[5]

9. You shall not lie.

10. Do not long for[6] other people's things.

(Exod. 20:1-17)

1 swear: to use words that are deliberately rude and offensive 욕하다

2 curse:

3 Sabbath Day:

4 adultery:

5 steal:

6 long for:

Write the Ten Commandments for Yourself!

이제 십계명을 외워볼까요? 외운 후 다음 빈칸에 십계명을 써보세요.

1.

2.

3.

4.

5.

6.

7.

8.

9.

10.

Moses and The Ten Commandments

(to the tune 'I'll tell me ma')

TEN ~ Don't envy.

NINE ~ Don't lie.

EIGHT ~ Don't look around with thievin' eyes.

SEVEN ~ Be faithful.

SIX ~ Don't kill.

FIVE ~ Honour parents: show good will.

FOUR ~ The Sabbath is a holy day.

Six days work now it's time to play.

THREE ~ TWO ~ ONE ~ are all to do

with loving God 'cos He loves you.

(instrumental)

THREE ~ Respect God's holy name.

TWO ~ No idols be your shame.

ONE ~ No other God obey.

Let these laws guide you today.

(instrumental)

Repeat the whole song

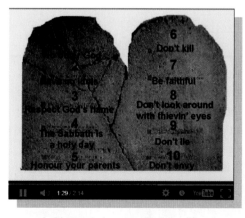

used with permission www.sheilahamil.co.uk

Mini Test ② Class _____ Name _____

A Dictation Test 🎧 08-8

- 오디오를 듣고 단어를 받아쓰세요. 단어는 각각 세 번씩 들려드립니다.

01 _____   02 _____   03 _____

04 _____   05 _____   06 _____

07 _____   08 _____   09 _____

10 _____   11 _____   12 _____

- 오디오를 듣고 다음 문장을 받아쓰세요. 문장은 세 번 들려드립니다.

13 I _____ _____ _____ ____ _____ ___ _____ ____ .

B Reading Comprehension Test

- 다음 인물에 적합한 설명을 아래 보기에서 골라 쓰세요.

01 Isaac _____   02 Rebekah _____

03 Jacob _____   04 Esau _____

05 Joseph _____   06 Reuben _____

07 Moses _____   08 Aaron _____

(a) I was discovered and raised by Pharaoh's daughter.
(b) I sold my birthright to my younger brother for a meal of lentil stew and bread.
(c) I was called to interpret Pharaoh's dreams.
(d) I was almost sacrificed by my father, but God sent a ram to take my place.
(e) I was sought out by a servant to be Isaac's wife.
(f) I was the first priest of Israel.
(g) At Panel, my name was changed to "Israel" after I wrestled with God in the form of a man.
(h) I prevented my younger brothers from killing Joseph.

Grammar Test

01 다음 문장 중에서 완전 자동사(verb intransitive)가 아닌 것은?

(a) The servant left the next day.

(b) They were in the field.

(c) Rebekah was a sister of Laban.

(d) He is walking to the park.

02 다음의 문장을 보기처럼 바꿔보세요.

> **보기**
>
> Mom sent me a letter. → Mom sent a letter to me.

(a) I will lend Minhee some money.

→ _____

(b) I will give Mom a birthday present.

→ _____

03 다음 문장 중에서 틀린 부분을 찾아 고쳐보세요. 틀린 부분이 없을 경우 X라고 쓰세요.

(a) Can you lent to me it?

(b) Mom had Dad to change the light bulb.

(c) I'll let Minju call you.

(d) I saw him to walk into the park.

(e) Dad can't hear the phone ringing.

04 다음 말에 대해 적절하게 답변해 보세요.

A: I have studied English for more than three years. But I am still poor at English.

B: _____

Bible Crossword

모세와 아론이 바로 앞에 가서 '내 백성을 보내라'는 하나님의 말씀을 전했을 때 바로가 이를 받아들이지 않아 하나님께서 열 가지의 재앙을 보냅니다. 다음은 그 재앙들 중 여덟 가지입니다. 가로 세로 힌트를 보며 퍼즐을 풀어보세요!

TEN PLAGUES

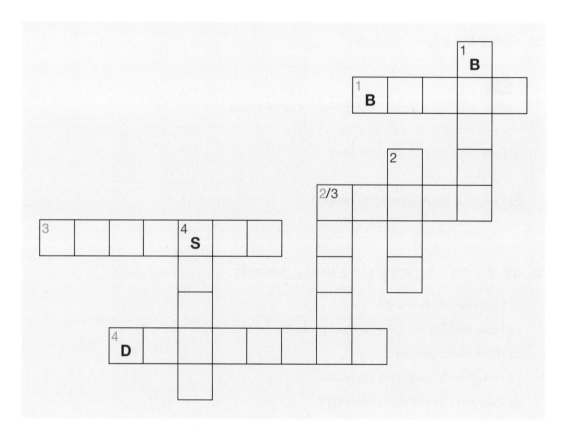

정답 ▶ p. 174

106

ACROSS

1 The Nile River turned into ☐☐☐☐☐.

2 The second plague was to fill the land with ☐☐☐☐☐.

3 ☐☐☐☐☐☐☐. large insects that live mainly in hot countries

4 ☐☐☐☐☐☐☐☐. the opposite of light

DOWN

1 ☐☐☐☐☐. a red, painful swelling on the skin containing thick, yellow liquid

2 The final plague was to kill the first ☐☐☐☐ Egyptian child.

3 ☐☐☐☐☐. black, dirty small insects

4 ☐☐☐☐☐. a lot of rain, sometimes with lightning or thunder

Question!　　What is the most dreadful plague in your eyes?

promised Land

09

Moses' Aide and Successor

Then Moses summoned Joshua and said to him in the presence of all Israel, "Be strong and courageous, for you must go with this people into the land that the LORD swore to their forefathers to give them, and you must divide it among them as their inheritance. (Deut. 31:7)

Who Am I?

STEP 1 Listen!

오디오를 듣고 말하고 있는 인물이 누구인지 알아맞혀 보세요.

A

🎧 09-1

Who am I?

✎

B

🎧 09-2

✎

Who am I?

STEP 2 Speak!

오디오를 듣고 큰소리로 따라 읽어 보세요.

  09-3

 ## Joshua: Moses' Aide[1] and Successor

Joshua means 'Yahweh is salvation.'[2]

At the time of the Exodus, he was "an aide to Moses." (Exod. 24:13)

Joshua helped defeat[3] Amalek and went with Moses to Mount Sinai.

Twelve men including him were sent into Jericho to spy[4] on it.

Among them, only Joshua and Caleb brought back a favorable report.

After the death of Moses, he became the leader of the Israelites.

He led the Israelites into the Promised Land, fighting many battles.[5]

The battle of Jericho made him famous as a sincere Christian warrior.[6]

He conquered the Promised Land and divided it up among the twelve tribes of Israel.

His farewell speech to the Israelites was well-known as a warning[7] not to forget God.

He was dead at the age of 110.

Words and Idioms | Consult the index dictionary if needed.

1 aide: someone whose job is to help another person in their work 보조자, 조력자
....

2 salvation:
....

3 defeat:
....

4 spy:
....

5 battle:
....

6 warrior:
....

7 warning:
....

 ## Rahab: The Brave Prostitute

Rahab was living in Jericho.

She had to work as a prostitute[1] to support[2] her family.

She hid the two Israelite spies from the king.

She heard about the power of the Israelite God and believed in Him.

She helped two Israelites escape by letting them down by a rope through the window

because her house was part of the great wall.

In return,[3] she could spare her family's lives.

The scarlet[4] rope in the window was the sign.

She married to Salmon and had a son named Boaz.

One of her descendants is David.

She was famous as a woman who put her belief into action.[5]

Words and Idioms | Consult the index dictionary if needed.

1 prostitute: someone, especially a woman, who is paid to have sex with people 창녀

2 support:

3 in return:

4 scarlet:

5 put one's belief into action:

동사의 종류 (Verbs 6): 형식별 동사 총정리

지금까지 다양한 동사의 형태에 대해 공부했습니다. 이번 장에서는 동사의 종류를 종합적으로 정리해보는 시간을 가져보겠습니다. 학교에서 배우는 문법인 5형식의 형태로 동사를 정리해보죠.

문장의 5형식

1. **1형식: 주어 + 동사(완전 자동사, verb intransitive)**

   God always **walks** with Joseph.
   └ 동사가 주어의 동작을 완전하게 설명함

2. **2형식: 주어 + 동사(불완전 자동사, linking verb) + 보어(명사 혹은 형용사)**

   ⌐ 동사 '~이다'로는 뜻의 전달이 완전히 안 됨

   Esau **is** the elder brother of Jacob.
   주어 Esau를 보충 설명하는 명사 보어(Complement)

   She **is** intelligent.
   형용사 보어

3. **3형식: 주어 + 동사(완전 타동사, verb transitive) + 목적어(명사)**

   God **set** a beautiful rainbow in the sky.
   동사   목적어(~을/를로 해석)

4. **4형식: 주어 + 동사(수여동사) + 간접목적어(~에게) + 직접목적어(~을/를)**

   Minji **showed** me her field trip pictures.
   ~에게   ~을(를)

   = Minji showed her field trip pictures to me.

5. **5형식: 주어 + 동사 + 목적어 + 목적보어**

   Joseph **helped** Pharaoh save Egypt from starvation.
   목적어   목적보어

   ▶ 굶주림에서 구하는 일을 하는 사람은 바로 왕

 Exercise 밑줄 친 부분이 각각 몇 형식 동사로 쓰인 것인지 적어보세요.

1 Don't <u>call</u> me Naomi.

2 Can you <u>give</u> me some water?

3 I <u>was</u> at home last night.

4 That cake <u>tastes</u> good.

5 Isaac <u>loved</u> his first son.

A Let's Memorize the Patterns! 09-5

'~을 듣다'라는 뜻을 지닌 동사 hear는 about, from, of 등의 전치사와 함께 사용되는 경우도 있습니다. 구체적인 상황을 구분하는 것이 약간 힘들지만, 일상생활에서 말할 때는 매우 유용하므로 문장 형태를 통째로 외워주세요.

- hear about something ~에 대해 소식을 듣다
  ▶ 상대방이 알고 있다고 생각하고 말할 때

- hear of someone or something ~가 있다는 것(존재)을 듣다
  ▶ 상대방이 모르고 있다고 생각되는 얘기를 꺼낼 때

- hear from someone ~에게 연락을 받다

편하게 말할 경우(informal speech) hear about과 hear of는 거의 구별 없이 사용되고 있으며, 문맥에 따라 달리 해석합니다.

A: Did you **hear about** Minji? 민지에 대한 소식 들었니? ▶ B가 민지를 아는 경우
B: No, what happened to her? 아니. 민지에게 무슨 일 있니?

A: Have you **heard of** PSY? 싸이에 대해 들어본 적이 있니? ▶ B가 싸이를 모르는 경우
B: No, I have never **heard of** PSY. Who is he? 아니. 싸이에 대해 들어본 적이 없어. 그가 누구야?

I just **heard from** Minsun. She is in New York.
민선이한테 방금 연락을 받았어. 뉴욕에 있대.

B Let's Talk: Pair Work

두 명씩 한 조를 만들어 보세요. 그런 후 다음에 제시된 문장을 사용하여 서로 영어로 대화해 보세요.

1	Partner A	Have you heard from _____?
	Partner B	No, I haven't heard from _____ in three years.
	or	Yes, I just met _____ at the theater.
2	Partner A	I have never heard of _____. Have you eaten any?
	Partner B	No/Yes, _____.

A My Confession 🎧 09-6

At the time of the Exodus, Joshua was always a faithful assistant to Moses. Joshua helped defeat the enemies at the attack by Amalek. He even went to the mountain of God with Moses. Even though he witnessed the huge numbers of warriors in Jericho, he still believed that God would help the Israelites defeat them. While Moses was leading the Israelites out of Egypt and wandering in the wilderness, Joshua always helped Moses as a second-in-command. This faithfulness and sincerity would make Joshua the successor to Moses when he died. This could also let Joshua enter and take over the Promised Land. Can you be the person like Joshua whose faith had never been shaken as a second-in-command? Share your idea with group members and write down your idea in English if possible.

출애굽기 시절에 여호수아는 항상 모세의 충실한 조력자였습니다. 여호수아는 모세를 도와 아말렉의 공격을 무찔렀습니다. 모세와 함께 시내산에도 올라갔죠. 여리고에서는 엄청난 수의 병사들을 목격했지만 여전히 하나님께서 이스라엘 백성들을 도와 그들을 무찌를 것이라 믿었습니다. 모세가 이스라엘 백성들을 애굽에서 데리고 나와 광야에서 방황할 때도 여호수아는 2인자로서 모세를 항상 도왔습니다. 이런 충실함과 신실성 때문에 여호수아는 모세가 죽자 그의 계승자가 될 수 있었습니다. 이 때문에 또한 여호수아는 약속된 땅에 들어가 이 지역을 점령할 수 있었습니다. 여러분은 2인자로서 신앙이 결코 흔들리지 않는 여호수아 같은 사람이 될 수 있나요? 다른 친구들과 이야기를 나누어 본 후 여러분의 생각을 가능하면 영어로 써보세요.

 영어로 쓰기가 힘들다면 우리말로 써도 괜찮습니다.

B Let's Pray! 🎧 09-7

때때로 여러분도 소리 없이 하나님의 일을 할 때가 있을 겁니다. 아무도 알아주지 않아도 하나님께서 여러분을 지켜보시고 돌보신다는 걸 꼭 기억하세요. 여호수아가 약속된 땅에 들어갈 수 있었던 것도 바로 그런 참고 견디었던 믿음 때문이 아닌가 하네요. 다음은 여호수아의 믿음을 본받아 자신도 그럴 것이라 고백하며 하나님의 돌보심을 기원하는 기도입니다.

Dear Lord, Joshua was second to Moses, but he always believed that You walked with him. He trusted in You and You brought the Israelites to the Promised Land, as You said. I will always trust in You as Joshua did. I believe you will always look after me throughout my life. Amen.	사랑의 주님. 여호수아는 2인자였습니다. 하지만 당신이 함께 하심을 항상 믿었습니다. 여호수아는 주님을 믿었고, 주님께서는 당신이 말씀하신대로, 약속된 땅으로 이스라엘 백성을 안내하셨습니다. 여호수아가 그랬던 것처럼 저도 주님을 항상 믿을 것입니다. 제 삶 가운데 주님께서 항상 저를 돌봐주실 것을 믿습니다. 아멘.

┌─────────────────────────────┐
│ Write a Prayer for Yourself! │
└─────────────────────────────┘

이제 여러분만의 믿음을 고백하는 기도를 해볼까요? 위의 예처럼 간단하게 영어로 기도를 써보세요.

Dear Lord,

Amen.

God's words to Joshua

(to the tune 'In and Out Those Dusty Bluebells')

I'll not leave you nor forsake you.
To a good land, I will take you.
If you're brave then I'll repay you.
I am the Master.

Tippy tippy tap tap, come be bolder,
Tippy tippy tap, lean on my shoulder,
Tippy tippy, let my arms enfold you.
I will be with you.

Keep the laws that Moses gave you,
don't turn right or left. I pray you'll
keep them, all for they will save you.
I am the Master.

Tippy tippy tap tap, come be bolder,
Tippy tippy tap, lean on my shoulder,
Tippy tippy, let my arms enfold you.
I will be with you.

Will you let my words enrich you?
Act them out and let them teach you?
Then success will surely reach you.
I am the Master.

Tippy tippy tap tap, come be bolder,
Tippy tippy tap, lean on my shoulder,
Tippy tippy, let my arms enfold you.
I will be with you. (x2)

used with permission www.sheilahamil.co.uk

The Idol Breaker in the Age of Judges

So that day they called Gideon "Jerub-Baal," saying, "Let Baal contend with him,"

because he broke down Baal's altar. (Judg. 6:32)

STEP 1 Listen!

오디오를 듣고 말하고 있는 인물이 누구인지 알아맞혀 보세요.

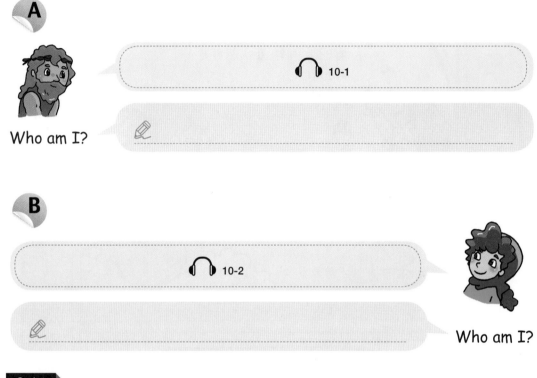

A

🎧 10-1

Who am I?

B

🎧 10-2

Who am I?

A | I was the fifth judge of Israel. When the angel of the Lord asked me to save the Israelites from the Midianites, I protested His order. My social position and power were very weak at that time. I asked God to give me a sign. After receiving the signs from God, I decided to be the leader of the Israelites. Sometimes I was called "Jerubbaal" because I broke down my family's idol, Baal. In order to fight the Midianites, I gathered many thousands of Israelite soldiers, but God permitted me only 300 men. On God's instructions, we defeated enemies only by blowing on the trumpets and throwing down the lamps. I regret setting up an ephod (idol) instead of accepting the kingship. Who am I?

B | My name means "bee." I was the fourth judge of Israel. I was the only female judge mentioned in the Bible. I was also 'a prophetess' and 'a mother in Israel.' I held court and settled the disputes of the Israelites. I went to Barak and told him that God called him to fight Sisera, the commander of the enemies. But Barak insisted that I go with him. Barak and I gathered an army to attack Sisera. When the battle started, God sent the heavy rain. So we attacked the sinking chariots and won the victory. With the help of the brave foreign woman, Jael, we caused the death of Sisera. I am famous for a song I sang in battle. Who am I?

STEP 2

오디오를 듣고 큰소리로 따라 읽어 보세요.

 10-3

 Gideon: The Idol[1] Breaker

Gideon was the fifth judge of Israel.

When the angel of the Lord asked him to save the Israelites from the Midianites, he protested His order.

He thought his social position[2] and power were very weak at that time.

He asked God to give him a sign.

After receiving the signs from God, he decided to be the leader of the Israelites.

Sometimes he was called "Jerubbaal" because he broke down his family's idol, Baal.

In order to fight the Midianites, he gathered many thousands of Israelite soldiers, but God permitted[3] him only 300 men.

On God's instructions, the Israelite soldiers defeated enemies only by blowing on the trumpets and throwing down the lamps.

He set up an ephod[4] (idol) instead of accepting the kingship.[5]

- **Midian**: Midian was located in the northwestern part of Arabia and its leaders oppressed the Israelites for 7 years.

Words and Idioms | Consult the index dictionary if needed.

1 idol: a picture or statue that is worshipped as a god 우상

2 position: ....

3 permit: ....

4 ephod: ....

5 kingship: ....

 B 🎧 10-4

 ## Deborah: The Only Female Judge

Her name, Deborah, means "bee."

She was the fourth judge of Israel.

She was the only female judge mentioned in the Bible.

She was also 'a prophetess[1]' (Judg. 4:4) and 'a mother in Israel.' (Judg. 5:7)

She held court[2] and settled[3] the disputes[4] of the Israelites.

She went to Barak and told him that God called him to fight Sisera, the commander[5] of the enemies.

But Barak insisted that she go with him.

Deborah and Barak gathered an army to attack[6] Sisera.

When the battle started, God sent the heavy rain. So they attacked the sinking[7] chariots and won the victory.

With the help of the brave foreign[8] woman, Jael, they caused the death of Sisera.

She is famous for a song she sang in battle.

| Words and Idioms | Consult the index dictionary if needed.

1 prophetess: a woman who is a prophet 여사제

2 court:

3 settle:

4 dispute:

5 commander:

6 attack:

7 sink:

8 foreign:

현재(Present)와 현재진행(Present Progressive) 시제

1. **현재 시제(Present Tense)**

   ❶ 현재의 습관적인 일을 말할 때 쓴다.

   I usually **go** to church <u>on Sundays</u>. 난 일요일마다 대개 교회에 가.
   빈도부사   시간을 나타내는 부사(구)

   ▶ 습관적인 일을 말할 때는 '빈도부사' 혹은 '시간을 나타내는 부사(구)'가 꼭 함께 쓰입니다.

   ❷ 절대적인 진리를 말할 때 쓴다.

   The earth **revolves** around the sun. 지구는 태양 주위를 돈다.

   ❸ 현재의 상태를 말할 때 쓴다

   I **am** a student. 나는 학생이다.

   ▶ 학생인 상태

2. **현재진행 시제(Present Progressive Tense)**

   '지금 말하는 바로 이 순간(at this moment)'에 어떤 일을 계속하고 있을 때 쓴다.

   I **am reading** the Bible now. 난 지금 성경을 읽고 있어.

   ▶ 말하는 지금 이 순간에 성경책을 읽고 있는 것

현재 시제와 현재진행 시제를 구분하는 가장 큰 기준은 시간을 나타내는 부사(구)입니다. 밑줄 친 부분을 참조하여 현재 시제와 현재진행 시제 중 빈칸에 적절한 동사의 형태를 써보세요.

1 I _____ (study) English every night.

2 She _____ (listen to) music right now.

3 Classes _____ (begin) in March.

4 I usually _____ (drink) milk once a day.

5 My cell phone _____ (beep). It's wake-up time.

이제 현재 시제와 현재진행 시제를 이용하여 간단한 문장을 만들어 볼까요?

1	지금 비가 오고 있다.	It _____.
2	나는 친구들과 자주 놀러 나간다. (go out)	I _____.
3	우리는 중학교 학생이다.	We _____.

A Let's Memorize the Patterns!   10-5

> • What do you do (for a living)?
>   ▶ 직업이나 직장을 물어보는 말(현재의 상태)
>   ▶ 이에 대한 대답은 〈I am + 직업명〉 또는 〈I work at + 장소〉
> • What are you doing (right now)?
>   ▶ 지금 하고 있는 일에 대해 물어보는 말
>   ▶ 이에 대한 대답은 〈I am + -ing〉

A: **What do you do (for a living)?** 무슨 일을 하세요?

B: **I am** a hairstylist. 미용사입니다.

or **I work at** a hair salon. 미용실에서 일해요.

A: **What are you doing now?** 지금 뭐해?

B: **I'm** watching TV. 텔레비전 보고 있어.

B Let's Talk: Pair Work

두 명씩 한 조를 만들어 보세요. 그런 후 다음에 제시된 문장을 사용하여 서로 영어로 대화해 보세요.

	Partner A What do you do (for a living)?	
	Partner B I am _____.	
1	*or* I work at _____.	
	직업의 종류 businessman 사업가 | professor 교수 | teacher 교사 | engineer 기술자 | firefighter 소방관 | minister 목사 | interior designer 실내장식가 | doctor 의사 | dentist 치과의사 | artist 예술가	
2	**Partner A** What are you doing now?	
	Partner B I am _____.	

 A   My Confession 🎧 10-6

Gideon gathered many Israelite soldiers together to fight against the Midianites. But God thought Gideon had too many soldiers. God said to him, "If your soldiers win the battle, they will boast of their mighty arms. I want them to know that I am the one who will lead them to win the battle." After that, God told Gideon to choose only 300 soldiers among them. The battle plan that God instructed was to let the soldiers blow their trumpets and throw down the lamps. And these instructions gave the Israelites the victory. Have you ever thought that you achieved your objective because you had enough abilities to do it? Have you ever forgot that God is always leading your life? Share your idea with group members and write down your idea in English if possible.

기드온은 미디안 병사들과 전투를 하기 위해 이스라엘 병사들을 많이 모집했습니다. 그러나 하나님은 기드온이 병사를 너무 많이 모집했다고 생각하셨죠. 하나님은 기드온에게 말씀하셨습니다. "네 병사들이 전투에서 이기면 자신들의 힘을 자랑할 것이다. 난 그들에게 전투를 승리로 이끈 자가 바로 나임을 알게 하고 싶다." 그런 후, 하나님은 기드온에게 그들 중 병사 300명만 선택하라고 하셨습니다. 하나님이 내린 명령이란 군인들에게 나팔을 불고 횃불을 던지게 하는 것이었습니다. 그리고 이러한 하나님의 명령으로 이스라엘 백성들은 승리했습니다. 여러분은 자신의 능력으로만 목적을 이루었다고 생각한 적이 있나요? 하나님께서 항상 여러분의 삶을 이끄신다는 것을 잊어본 적이 있나요? 다른 친구들과 이야기를 나누어 본 후 여러분의 생각을 가능하다면 영어로 써보세요.

 영어로 쓰기가 힘들다면 우리말로 써도 괜찮습니다.

B Let's Pray! 🎧 10-7

사사기 5장에 나오는 '드보라의 찬가'(The Song of Deborah)는 매우 사랑받는 찬가 중 하나입니다. 다음은 12절로 드보라와 바락의 사기를 높이는 노래입니다. 큰 소리로 읽으며, 그 마음을 느껴보세요.

Wake up, wake up, Deborah!	깰지어다, 깰지어다, 드보라여!
Wake up, wake up, break out in song!	깰지어다, 깰지어다, 너는 노래할지어다!
Arise, O Barak!	일어날지어다, 바락이여!
Take captive your captives, O son of Abinoam!	네가 사로잡은 자를 끌고 갈지어다, 아비노암의 아들이여!
(Judg. 5:12)	(사사기 5:12)

┌─────────────────────┐
│ Deborah in My Mind! │
└─────────────────────┘

여러분의 머릿속에 있는 드보라를 그려보세요. 그런 후, 왜 이런 모습을 그리게 되었는지 영어로 간단하게 써보세요.

She

Gideon, Mighty Warrior

(to the tune 'The Grand Old Duke of York')

And God said to Gideon, *"You have too many men,*
pick out all the fearful ones, and send them home again!
I want their spirits up, can't use those feeling down.
I want no soldiers 'half-way' up, for they're neither up nor down!"

Then God said to Gideon, *"You've still too many men!*
Take them all to the water's edge, have them drink and then,
watch those who are lapping up, observe who's kneeling down,
and choose for me the watchful ones, alert and looking round!"

The enemy camp below them, lay on the valley floor
God sent a friend with Gideon to listen at their door.
They heard some whispered fears, that death was all around,
So Gideon knew the time was right for a full and out showdown.

So in the dead of night, three hundred men he led,
in silence to the enemy camp, while they were still in bed.

He planned to wake them up; he was going to break them down.
He was going to give them such a shock, they'd run right out of town.

The enemy camp was big and stretched as far as eye could see.
With horns and torches, Gideon's men yelled out eerily,
"A SWORD FOR THE LORD AND GIDEON!"
The enemy they woke up, their world was upside down.
They turned and killed each other, and they fell upon the ground.
But a few fled from the town!
Gideon's men soon tracked them down!

"A SWORD FOR THE LORD AND GIDEON!"

used with permission www.sheilahamil.co.uk

The Man with More-than-human Strength

So he told her everything. "No razor has ever been used on my head," he said, "because I have been a Nazirite set apart to God since birth. If my head were shaved, my strength would leave me, and I would become as weak as any other man." (Judg. 16:17)

Who Am I?

STEP 1 Listen!

오디오를 듣고 말하고 있는 인물이 누구인지 알아맞혀 보세요.

A

🎧 11-1

Who am I?

✏️

B

🎧 11-2

✏️

Who am I?

A | I was a judge. I was chosen to serve the Lord and deliver Israel from the Philistines. I had been forbidden by God to cut my hair since Mom conceived me. When I was a boy, I was much stronger than the other children of my age. I even killed a lion with my hands. I fell in love with a woman from the valley of Sorek, but I was tricked by her into telling the secret of my strength. She cut my hair, and I lost my great strength. I was sent to prison by the Philistines. But my strength was restored when my hair grew long again. When I was called to entertain people at the feast, I pushed down two supporting pillars and died with about 3000 Philistines. Who am I?

B | I was from the valley of Sorek. An Israelite man with superhuman power fell in love with me. At that time, the rulers of the Philistines visited me and said, "Find out what makes him so strong. We will give you lots of money." I agreed, and my appealing for love made him tell me the secret of his strength. While the strong Israelite was sleeping on my lap, I called a man to shave off seven braids of his hair. I let the Philistines in to bind him. After that I disappeared in the story. But some great poets like John Milton and musicians like Camille Saint-Saëns made me known as a quite coquettish and sensual woman. Who am I?

STEP 2 `Speak!`

오디오를 듣고 큰소리로 따라 읽어 보세요.

  11-3

 Samson: The Man with More-than-human Strength

Samson was a judge.

He was chosen to serve the Lord and deliver[1] Israel from the Philistines.

He had been forbidden[2] by God to cut his hair since his mother conceived[3] him.

When he was a boy, he was much stronger than the other children of his age.

He even killed a lion with his hands.

He fell in love with a woman named Delilah who was from the valley of Sorek.

He was tricked by her into telling the secret[4] of his strength.

Delilah cut his hair, and Samson lost his great strength.

He was sent to the prison by Philistines.

His strength was restored[5] when his hair grew long again.

When he was called to entertain[6] the people at the feast, he pushed down two supporting pillars[7] and died with about 3000 Philistines.

• **Sorek**: Sorek is located within the Israelite land of Canaan, not far from Jerusalem.

`Words and Idioms` Consult the index dictionary if needed.

1 deliver: to free someone from an unpleasant situation 구하내다

2 forbid: ....   **3 conceive:** ....

4 secret: ....   **5 restore:** ....

6 entertain: ....   **7 pillar:** ....

Delilah: Woman from the Valley[1] of Sorek

Delilah was from the valley of Sorek.

Samson fell in love with her.

The rulers of the Philistines visited her and said, "Find out what makes him so strong.

We will give you lots of money," and she agreed.

Her appealing[2] for love made Samson tell the secret of his strength.

While Samson was sleeping on her lap,[3] she called a man to shave off seven braids[4] of

his hair (Judg. 16:19).

She let the Philistines in to bind[5] Samson.

She disappeared in the story after Samson's head was shaved, but some great poets

like John Milton and musicians like Camille Saint-Saëns made her known as a quite

coquettish[6] and sensual[7] woman.

Words and Idioms | Consult the index dictionary if needed.

1 valley: a low area of land between two mountains or hills, usually with a river flowing through it 계곡

2 appealing: **3** lap:

4 braid: **5** bind:

6 coquettish: **7** sensual:

과거(Past)와 과거진행(Past Progressive) 시제

1. **과거 시제(Past Tense)**

   ❶ 과거에 일어난 일을 말할 때 쓴다. 이미 끝난 행동임을 꼭 기억할 것.

   I **walked** to school yesterday.

   　　　　　　　　　'어제'는 과거

   [비교] I **walk** to school every day. (현재 시제)

   　　　　　　　　　'매일'은 습관적인 동작을 말하므로 현재

   ❷ 과거를 말하는 대표적인 부사: last, ago

   ▶ **last + 명사** 지난 ~

   ▶ **시간을 나타내는 명사(구) + ago** ~전에

   I **went** there **last** night.

   　　　　　　지난밤에

   I **finished** my homework ten minutes **ago**.

   　　　　　　　　　　　　　10분 전에

2. **과거진행 시제(Past Progressive Tense)**

   과거의 어떤 한 순간에 일정 행동을 진행하고 있을 때 쓴다.

   　　　　　　　　　　　　　　↗ 네가 전화했을 때(순간)

   I **was** play**ing** the violin when you **called** me.

   ↘ 바이올린을 켜고 있었음(일정 기간 동작을 하고 있음)

   While Samson **was** sleep**ing** on her lap, she **called** a man to shave

   　　　　　　일정 기간 자고 있었음　　　　　　데릴라가 남자를 부른 순간

   off seven braids of his hair.

 **Exercise** 주어진 동사를 과거 혹은 과거진행형으로 써서 빈칸을 채워보세요.

1 A: What _____ (you, do)?

B: Doing? When?

A: Last morning around 11.

B: I _____ (run) in the park at that time.

2 A: What _____ (you, do) last night?

I _____ (call) you a hundred times!

B: Did you? I _____ (sleep) early last night.

A Let's Memorize the Patterns! 11-5

삼손이 힘을 잃은 것은 머리카락이 잘렸기 때문입니다. 본문에서 삼손에게는 shave the head라는 표현을 썼지만 정확하게 말하자면 이 표현은 우리가 생각하는 '머리를 자르다'는 아닙니다. 이때는 cut the hair 혹은 have a haircut이라는 표현을 쓰죠. 이 표현이 어떻게 다른지 한번 볼까요?

- shave the head 머리를 빡빡 밀다
- cut one's hair ~의 머리를 깎다
- have/get(need) a haircut 머리를 깎다(깎을 필요가 있다)

They **shaved their head** to express their anger.
그들은 분노를 표현하기 위해 머리를 빡빡 밀었다.

The weather is getting hot. I want to **cut my hair short**.
날씨가 더워지고 있어요. 머리를 짧게 깎고 싶어요.

My hair is bushy. I **need a haircut**.
머리가 덥수룩해요. 머리를 깎아야겠어요.

B Let's Talk: Pair Work

두 명씩 한 조를 만들어 보세요. 그런 후 다음에 제시된 문장을 가능하면 암기해서 서로 대화해 보세요.

1	**Partner A** I want to cut my hair short. **Partner B** (hairdresser): How much do you want to cut off? **Partner A** Shoulder length, please. *or* (손으로 가리키며) I like this length.
2	**Partner A** You did something to your hair. **Partner B** I got a haircut. **Partner A** Your hair suits you.

Confession & Prayer

 A **My Confession** 🎧 11-6

Samson was a blessed judge in that he was chosen to serve the Lord and deliver the Israelites from the Philistines. Under the wings of God, he overpowered the Philistines. But he was very pathetic in relationship with women. Every woman that he fell in love with was forced to betray him. Delilah was even bribed by the Philistines and she tricked him into telling the secret of his superhuman strength. Delilah's betrayal made him lose his power. He was blinded by the Philistines and sent to prison. But God restored his strength. He answered Samson's final prayer to let him die with the Philistines. Do you believe that God always listens to your prayer even when you did bad things? Share your idea with group members and write down your idea in English if possible.

삼손은 하나님을 섬기고 이스라엘 사람들을 블레셋 사람들로부터 구원하도록 선택받았다는 점에서 매우 축복받은 사람입니다. 하나님의 보호 아래 삼손은 블레셋 사람들을 힘으로 이겼습니다. 그러나 여인들과의 관계에서 삼손은 매우 불쌍했습니다. 삼손이 사랑에 빠진 여성은 모두 그를 배반하도록 강압을 받았습니다. 심지어 들릴라는 블레셋 사람들에게 돈을 받고 삼손을 속여 그의 대단한 힘의 비밀을 알아냈습니다. 들릴라의 배신으로 삼손은 힘을 잃었습니다. 블레셋 사람들은 삼손의 눈을 멀게 하고 감옥에 보냈습니다. 하지만 하나님은 그의 힘을 다시 돌려주셨죠. 하나님은 블레셋 사람들과 함께 죽게 해달라는 삼손의 마지막 기도를 들어주셨습니다. 여러분은 여러분이 좋지 않은 행동을 했을 때도 하나님께서 늘 여러분의 기도에 귀를 기울이신다는 것을 믿나요? 다른 친구들과 이야기를 나누어 본 후 여러분의 생각을 가능하다면 영어로 써보세요.

 영어로 쓰기가 힘들다면 우리말로 써도 괜찮습니다.

B **Let's Pray!** 🎧 11-7

오늘은 진실로 나를 사랑해줄 사람을 만나게 해달라고 하나님께 기도해 볼까요?

Dear God,

Please lead me to the person in my life who will

truly love me.

사랑의 주님,

진실로 저를 사랑할 사람을 만나게 해주세요.

Write a Prayer for Yourself!

여러분이 생각하는 이상형(ideal type)은 어떤 사람인가요? 여러분이 생각하는 이상형을 묘사해 보세요. 가능하면 영어로 해보세요.

Samson and the Source of His Strength

(to tune 'Oh Dear, What Can the Matter Be?')

CHORUS:
Oh dear, what can the matter be?
Samson's girlfriend, Delilah, is here again,
asking his secret, but he smiles politely,
and he will not tell her, so there!

He told her the source of his strength was
in tying,
seven strong thongs round him; so then
she tried it.
While he was sleeping, the soldiers came
creeping.
*"SAMSON THE PHILISTINES ARE UPON
YOU!"*
But Samson, he just didn't care.
The real source of strength was his hair!
CHORUS: Oh dear...

He told her the source of his strength was
in tying,
some very new ropes round him; so then
she tried it.
While he was sleeping, the soldiers came
creeping.
*"SAMSON THE PHILISTINES ARE UPON
YOU!"*
But Samson, he just didn't care.
The real source of strength was his hair!
CHORUS: Oh dear...

He told her the source of his strength was
in weaving
the braids of his hair in a loom; so she
tried it.
While he was sleeping, the soldiers came
creeping,

*"SAMSON THE PHILISTINES ARE UPON
YOU!"*
But Samson, he just didn't care.
The real source of strength was his hair!
CHORUS: Oh dear...

He finally told her, she nagged him so
bitterly,
"Shave off my hair and my strength it will
leave me!"
So this she did, and she called out one last
time,
*"SAMSON THE PHILISTINES ARE UPON
YOU!"*
They blinded him, threw him in jail!
But that's not the end of the tale!

CHORUS TWO:
Oh dear what can the matter be?
Time has elapsed and his hair has grown
back again.
Got his revenge, by destroying the temple,
and killing his enemies there. Oh yeah!

used with permission www.sheilahamil.co.uk

12

The Faithful Daughter-in-law in Bethlehem

But Ruth replied, "Don't urge me to leave you or to turn back from you. Where you go I will go, and where you stay I will stay. Your people will be my people and your God my God." (Ruth 1:16) 📖

Who Am I?

STEP 1 Listen!

오디오를 듣고 말하고 있는 인물이 누구인지 알아맞혀 보세요.

A

🎧 12-1

Who am I?

✏️ _____

B

🎧 12-2

✏️ _____

Who am I?

142

STEP 2 Speak!

오디오를 듣고 큰소리로 따라 읽어 보세요.

  12-3

 ### Ruth: The Faithful Daughter-in-law in Bethlehem

Ruth was from Moab.

She married the second son of Naomi, who moved to Moab because of a famine.

Her family lived there happily for almost ten years, but her husband and brother-in-law passed away.[1]

Her mother-in-law, Naomi, decided to return to Bethlehem.

Naomi released[2] Ruth to go back to her family, but Ruth refused to leave her.

Ruth persuaded[3] Naomi to go together, saying "Where you go I will go, where you stay I will stay. Your people will be my people, and your God my God." (Ruth 1:16)

In Bethlehem, Naomi advised[4] Ruth to glean in Boaz' fields, a relative[5] to Naomi.

Boaz was a very kind and generous man.

Boaz helped Ruth in many ways and respected her.

Ruth got married to him, and they had a child named Obed, an ancestor of David.

• **gleaning**: In the days of Ruth, it was a custom[6] that the poor would follow behind the harvesters[7] and pick up any barley[8] left behind. It was called 'gleaning.'

Consult the index dictionary if needed.

1 pass away: to die 죽다아가다

2 release:

3 persuade:

4 advise:

5 relative:

6 custom:

7 harvester:

8 barley:

12-4

 ## Naomi: The Generous Mother-in-law

Naomi was a wife of Elimelech.

Naomi and her husband moved from their hometown, Bethlehem, to Moab because of a severe famine.

Her husband passed away and left her alone with two sons.

Her sons married Moabite women named Orpah and Ruth.

After her two sons died, Naomi did not want to live alone in a strange land, so she decided to return to her hometown.

She also released Orpah and Ruth to go back to their families, but Ruth strongly refused to leave her.

When Naomi met the women in Bethlehem, she asked them to call her "Mara" instead of Naomi because she thought God made her life bitter.[1] (Ruth 1:20)

In order to get food, she encouraged[2] Ruth to glean in Boaz' field.

When she noticed Boaz had a special feeling for her daughter-in-law, Naomi even encouraged her to get married to him.

Naomi lived happily with them after Ruth and Boaz got married.

Words and Idioms | Consult the index dictionary if needed.

1 bitter: making you feel very unhappy and upset 혹독한, 모진, 쓰라린

2 encourage:

과거 시제(Past Tense): 접속사 after, before를 사용할 때

두 문장을 연결하는 단어를 우리는 접속사(Conjunctive)라 부릅니다. 접속사 after와 before는 시간의 전후 관계를 나타낼 때 사용하는 대표적인 접속사이죠. 특히 과거의 일을 말할 때 after, before가 시간의 전후 관계를 분명히 결정해 줍니다.

> ↗ 먼저 일어났던 일(과거 시제)
> 1. After 주어1 + 동사1, 주어2 + 동사2
> ↘ 나중에 일어났던 일(과거 시제)
>
> ↗ 나중에 일어났던 일(과거 시제)
> 2. Before 주어1 + 동사1, 주어2 + 동사2
> ↘ 먼저 일어났던 일(과거 시제)
>
> ★ 과거의 일을 말할 때 먼저 일어난 일이 무엇인지 나중에 일어난 일이 무엇인지는 접속사 after/before만 봐도 알 수 있기 때문에, after/before절과 주절의 시제는 굳이 구분해 쓸 필요가 없답니다. after/before절과 주절 모두 과거 시제로 쓰면 된다는 점, 기억하세요!

Naomi **lived** happily with them **after** Ruth and Boaz **got** married.
       나중에 일어났던 일   먼저 일어났던 일
▶ 순서와 상관없이 동사의 시제가 모두 '과거 시제'라는 점 꼭 기억하세요.

I **finished** my homework **before** I **went** to a movie.
      먼저 일어났던 일   나중에 일어났던 일
▶ 순서와 상관없이 동사의 시제가 모두 '과거 시제'라는 점 꼭 기억하세요.

접속사 before와 after가 들어간 문장이 먼저 나올 경우 before/after가 이끄는 문장 뒤에 comma(,)를 써야 합니다.

After Ruth and Boaz got married, Naomi lived happily with them.
Before I went to a movie, I finished my homework.

Exercise 다음 두 문장을 접속사 before와 after를 사용해 연결해 보세요.

> **Example** I ate lunch at noon. I went to the library at 1:30 p.m.
> = After I ate lunch, I went to the library.
> = I ate lunch before I went to the library.

1 I turned off the TV at 9:30. I went to bed at 10:00.

= After _____.

= _____ before _____.

2 I took a shower at 7:00 a.m. I ate breakfast at 7:30 a.m.

= After _____.

= _____ before _____.

A Let's Memorize the Patterns! 12-5

우리말 '죽다'에 해당하는 영어 동사에는 die, pass away라는 두 가지 표현이 있습니다. die는 자신과 지위가 같거나 아래인 대상에게 씁니다. pass away는 높임말로 자신보다 지위나 나이가 높으신 분이 돌아가셨다고 할 때 쓰는 표현입니다.

- pass away 돌아가시다
  ▶ 자신보다 지위나 나이가 높으신 분이 돌아가셨을 때, 또는 공식적인 표현
- die 죽다

Her husband **passed away** and left her alone with two sons.
▶ 남편의 죽음을 높여서 표현하기 위해

Her two sons **died**.
▶ 나오미의 입장에서 아들은 아래 사람

B Let's Talk: Pair Work

두 명씩 한 조를 만들어 보세요. 그런 후 다음에 제시된 문장을 사용하여 서로 영어로 대화해 보세요.

1	Partner A	Do you live with (your grandmother) ?
	Partner B	No, she passed away (three years ago) .
2	Partner A	Why are you so down?
	Partner B	(My dog) died yesterday. I'm feeling down.

 A **My Confession** 12-6

Naomi decided to go back to her hometown and said to her daughters-in-law, "Each of you must go back to your mother's home. May the Lord show kindness to you." Orpah returned to her mother, but Ruth answered, "Where you go I will go, and where you stay I will stay. Your people will be my people and your God my God." As a Moabite widow, it would be very difficult for her to live with the Israelites. But Ruth chose the harder way. Even in hard circumstances, she continued to take care of her mother-in-law. And this faithfulness caused her to be accepted by God as one of His chosen people. Like Ruth, can you be faithful to your family in difficulties? Share your idea with your group members and write down your idea in English if possible.

나오미가 고향으로 돌아가기로 결심한 후 며느리들에게 말했습니다. "너희는 각자 고향으로 돌아가야만 한다. 하나님께서 너희를 돌봐주실 것이다." 오르바는 고향으로 돌아갔지만 룻은 "어머니께서 가시는 곳에 저도 가고 어머니께서 머무시는 곳에서 저도 머물겠나이다. 어머니의 백성이 저의 백성이 되고 어머니의 하나님이 저의 하나님이 되시리니."라고 답했죠. 모압 출신 미망인으로 이스라엘 사람들과 함께 사는 것은 매우 어려운 일이었을 텐데도, 룻은 그렇게 더 어려운 길을 선택했습니다. 힘든 환경에서도 룻은 시어머니를 계속 돌봐 드렸습니다. 그리고 바로 이런 신실함 때문에 룻은 하나님의 선택받은 자손으로 받아들여지게 되었던 것이죠. 룻처럼 여러분은 어려움 속에서도 여러분의 가족에게 충실할 수 있나요? 다른 친구들과 이야기를 나누어 본 후 가능하면 여러분의 생각을 영어로 써보세요.

 영어로 쓰기가 힘들다면 우리말로 써도 괜찮습니다.

B **Let's Pray!** 🎧 12-7

오늘은 우리에게 한없는 사랑을 주시는 부모님을 생각하며 감사기도를 해볼까요?

Dear God,

Thank you for Mom and Dad, who give me so
much, especially lots of love.

Help me show them that I love them too.

사랑의 하나님,

제게 특별히 한없는 사랑을 주시는 엄마, 아빠께
감사드립니다.

저 또한 두 분을 사랑한다는 걸 표현할 수 있도록
도와주세요.

Write a Prayer for Yourself!

이제 가족을 생각하며 여러분만의 기도를 해볼까요? 위의 예처럼 간단하게 영어로 기도를 써보
세요.

Dear Lord,

Amen.

Song of Ruth

(to the tune 'We Have Camp-fired Here')

My place is here,

right by your side.

Don't make me go,

here I will abide.

Where you go, I'll go, (echo)

where you stay, I'll stay. (echo)

Your people mine, (echo)

your God, my way. (echo)

And I'll love you, (echo)

till the very end. (echo)

Only death shall part us, (echo)

My one true friend. (echo)

(Repeat last two choruses)

**Where you go I'll go,
where you stay, I'll stay.**

used with permission www.sheilahamil.co.uk

13

The Attentive Listener to God Calling

The Lord came and stood there, calling as at the other times, "Samuel! Samuel!"

Then Samuel said, "Speak, for your servant is listening." (1 Sam. 3:10) 📖

Who Am I?

STEP 1 Listen!

오디오를 듣고 말하고 있는 인물이 누구인지 알아맞혀 보세요.

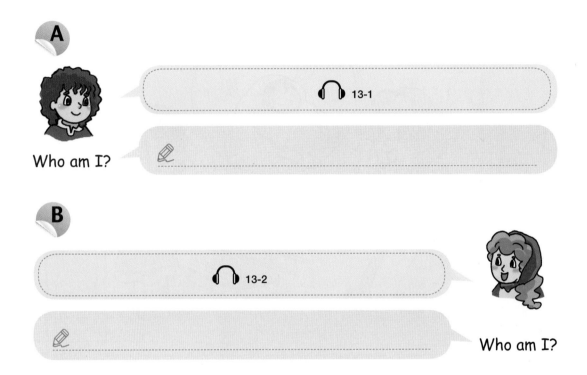

A

🎧 13-1

Who am I?

✏️

B

🎧 13-2

✏️

Who am I?

Script

A | I was dedicated by my mother to the Lord "as long as I live." When I was a baby, I was taken to the temple and raised by the priest Eli. When I was a young boy, I heard someone calling me. I lay asleep, so I thought Eli was calling. But it was God who called me. When God called me a fourth time, I answered, "Speak, for your servant is listening." (1 Sam. 3:9) God affirmed me as His prophet by calling me. In Acts 3:24, I was described as the first prophet. I was the last great judge of Israel as well. Because the Israelites demanded a king, I anointed Saul as king of Israel. I also anointed David as the second king of Israel. Who am I?

B | I was the wife of Elkanah. My husband loved me most even though he had another wife, Peninnah. She was jealous of me because Elkanah always gave me the best gifts. She said mean things about my childlessness. One day my family visited Shiloh. Peninnah treated me very badly, so I went to the temple in order to pray. In the temple, I prayed to God. "O Lord, if you will give me a son, then I will make him a special servant to you all his life." My prayer was answered. I was pregnant and had a son. As I promised to God, I gave my son as His servant when he was a baby. Who am I?

STEP 2 Speak!

오디오를 듣고 큰소리로 따라 읽어 보세요.

  13-3

 ### Samuel: The Attentive Listener to God Calling

Samel was dedicated[1] by his mother, Hannah, to the Lord all through his life.

When he was a baby, he was taken to the temple[2] and raised by the priest Eli.

When he was a young boy, he heard someone calling him.

He lay asleep, so he thought Eli was calling. But it was God who called him.

When God called him a fourth time, he answered, "Speak, for your servant is

listening."(1 Sam. 3:9)

God affirmed[3] him as His prophet by calling him.

In Acts 3:24, he was described as the first prophet.

He was the last great judge of Israel as well.[4]

He anointed[5] Saul as a king of Israel because the Israelites demanded a king.

He also anointed David as the second king of Israel.

| Words and Idioms | Consult the index dictionary if needed.

1 dedicate: to spend your time and effort doing something 헌신하다

2 temple: **3** affirm:

4 as well: **5** anoint:

 **B** 13-4

 Hannah: The Woman of Her Word

Hannah was the wife of Elkanah.

Her husband loved her most even though he had another wife, Peninnah.

Hannah was the object[1] of Penninah's envy because Elkanah always gave her the best gifts. So Penninah said mean things about her childlessness.

On a visit to Shiloh, Hannah was treated very badly by Peninnah. So she went to the temple in order to pray.

In the temple, she prayed to God. "O Lord, if You will give me a son, then I will make him a special servant to You all his life."

Her prayer was answered. She was pregnant[2] and had a son.

As she promised to God, she gave her son as His servant when he was a baby.

Words and Idioms Consult the index dictionary if needed.

1 object: the person that people have a particular feeling about

2 pregnant:

156

미래 시제(Future Tense): will과 be going to

미래 시제를 표현하는 대표적인 조동사(구)는 will과 be going to입니다. 이 두 조동사(구)는 모두 우리 말로 '~할 것이다'의 뜻을 가지고 있지만, 상황에 따라 쓰이는 때가 다른 경우도 있습니다.

1. will과 be going to를 모두 쓸 수 있는 경우

미래에 대한 예측이나 기대(expectation)를 나타낼 때는 will 또는 be going to를 쓰면 되죠. will과 be going to 뒤에는 모두 동사원형이 와야 합니다.

I think it **will/is going to** be rainy tomorrow. ▶ 비가 올 것을 예측
Minji **will/is going to** come home tomorrow. ▶ 민지가 내일 집에 올 것을 기대

2. be going to + 동사원형

확실하게 일정이 잡혔을 때는 be going to를 씁니다.

I'm going to meet Hyunjin for lunch at 12:30.
▶ 12시 30분에 확실히 현진이를 만나기로 예정된 경우

3. will + 동사원형

말하는 순간 어떤 것을 하겠다는 계획을 세웠을 때는 will을 씁니다. will에는 그 순간 말하는 사람의 의지가 담기게 되죠.

＾ 기대 혹은 예측(하나님께서 아들을 줄 것이라는)
If you **will** give me a son, then I **will** make him a special servant to you all his life.
＼ 말하는 순간의 결심(하나님께 아들을 바치겠음)

Exercise 적절한 동사형을 선택하세요. 두 개가 모두 옳으면 모두 선택하세요.

1 We (are going to / will) go to the movie tonight.

2 A: Let's talk again tomorrow.

B: Okay, (I'm going to call / I'll call) you tonight.

3 I think it (is going to / will) be sunny this weekend.

4 I (am going to / will) be ready in a minute.

5 He (is going to / will) graduate this year.

A Let's Memorize the Patterns! 13-5

동사 treat는 '대접하다'의 뜻을 가지고 있습니다. 특히 누구를 대접하거나, 돈을 낼 때 이 treat란 동사는 유용하게 쓰입니다.

- 주어 + treat + 사람 ~를 대접하다
- 주어 + treat + 사람 + to + 장소 ~를 …에 초대하다

Hannah **was treated** very badly. 한나는 매우 푸대접을 받았다.

I've **never been treated** that way. 나는 그렇게 푸대접을 받은 적은 없었다.

He **treated me to the movies**. 그는 내게 영화를 보여주었다.
　　　　　사람　　　to 장소

Let me **treat** you. 제가 낼게요.

B Let's Talk: Pair Work

두 명씩 한 조를 만들어 보세요. 그런 후 다음에 제시된 문장을 사용하여 서로 영어로 대화해 보세요.

1	Partner A	How was your date?
	Partner B	It was really bad. I'd never been treated that way before.
2	Partner A	Let me treat you.
	Partner B	No, you paid for it last time. This time, it's on me.
		★ It's on me. 내가 낼게.
3	Partner A	I'll treat you to the movie.
	Partner B	No, not tonight. I have to finish English homework.

Confession & Prayer

 A   My Confession 🎧 13-6

In those days when the boy Samuel ministered under Eli, "the word of the LORD was rare." (1 Sam. 3:1) Even the judge, Eli, could not hear God's words. In the dark one night, Samuel heard a voice calling him. Samuel ran to the Eli's room and said "Here I am. You called me." Eli did not call him. When Samuel ran to Eli a third time, Eli realized that the LORD was calling the boy. So he told Samuel, "If he calls you again, say, Speak, LORD, for your servant is listening." When Samuel responded to God's calling, he received a message from God. What do you think made Samuel listen to God calling? Do you think he could listen because he was ready to hear God calling? Are you also ready for listening to God calling? Share your idea with your group members and write down your idea in English if possible.

어린 사무엘이 엘리 밑에서 하나님을 섬겼던 시절에, 하나님의 말씀은 거의 없었습니다.(사무엘상 3:1) 제사장인 엘리조차 하나님의 말씀을 들을 수 없었습니다. 그러던 어느 날 한 밤중에 사무엘은 자신을 부르는 목소리를 들었습니다. 사무엘은 엘리의 방으로 달려가, "저를 부르셨기로 제가 여기 있나이다."라고 말했습니다. 엘리는 그를 부르지 않았습니다. 사무엘이 엘리에게 세 번째 달려갔을 때, 엘리는 하나님께서 이 아이를 부르고 있다는 것을 깨달았습니다. 그러자 엘리는 사무엘에게, "그분께서 너를 부르시거든 네가 말하기를 여호와여 말씀하옵소서. 주의 종이 듣겠나이다." 하라고 말했습니다. 사무엘이 하나님의 부름에 답했을 때 그는 말씀을 받았습니다. 왜 사무엘은 하나님의 부르심을 들었을까요? 들을 준비가 되어서 들었던 것이 아닐까요? 여러분도 하나님의 부르심을 들을 준비가 되어 있나요? 다른 친구들과 이야기를 나눠 본 후 가능하면 여러분의 생각을 영어로 써보세요.

 영어로 쓰기가 힘들다면 우리말로 써도 괜찮습니다.

B Let's Pray! 🎧 13-7

한나는 사무엘을 여호와께 바친 후에 여호와를 찬양하는 기도를 드렸습니다. 다음은 한나의 기도 중 일부입니다. 가능하다면 암기해보는 것이 어떨까요?

My heart rejoices[1] in the LORD;

in the LORD my horn[2] is lifted[3] high.

My mouth boasts[4] over my enemies,[5]

for I delight in your deliverance.[6]

There is no one holy like the LORD

there is no one besides you;

there is no Rock like our God.

(1 Sam. 2:1-2)

내 마음이 여호와로 말미암아 즐거워하며

내 뿔이 여호와로 말미암아 높아졌으며

내 입이 내 원수들을 향하여 크게 열렸으니

이는 내가 주의 구원으로 말미암아 기뻐함이니이다.

여호와와 같이 거룩하신 이가 없으시니

이는 주밖에 다른 이가 없고

우리 하나님 같은 반석이 없으심이니이다.

(사무엘상 2:1-2)

| Words and Idioms | Consult the index dictionary if needed.

1 rejoice: to feel very happy about something 기뻐하다, 좋아하다

2 horn:

3 lift:

4 boast:

5 enemy:

6 deliverance:

God Calls Samuel

(to the tune 'Rock a Bye Baby')

'Samuel! Samuel!'

"Here I am, Eli,
You called me!" he said.
The old man woke up
and he stared straight ahead.

"I didn't call you,
Samuel, instead
go back to your room
and lie down in your bed!"

'Samuel! Samuel!'

"Here I am, Eli,
You called me!" he said.
The old man woke up again
rubbed his old head.

"I didn't call you,
Samuel, instead
go back to your room,
and lie down in your bed!"

'Samuel! Samuel!'

"Here I am, Eli,
you called me!" he said.
The old man then knew
it was God's voice he heard.

"Next time young Samuel
speak out and don't fear.
Say 'Speak Lord, I am listening!'
Your servant is here!"

used with permission www.sheilahamil.co.uk

Mini Test ③

Class _____   Name _____

A Dictation Test 🎧 13-8

■ 오디오를 듣고 단어를 받아쓰세요. 단어는 각각 세 번씩 들려드립니다.

01 _____   02 _____   03 _____

04 _____   05 _____   06 _____

07 _____   08 _____   09 _____

10 _____

■ 오디오를 듣고 다음 문장을 받아쓰세요. 문장은 세 번 들려드립니다.

11 W_____ _____ _____ _____ ___ _____ _____, ____ _____,

"_____, ____ _____ _____ ___ _____."

B Reading Comprehension Test

■ 다음 인물에 적합한 설명을 아래 보기에서 골라 쓰세요.

01 Joshua   _____   02 Rahab   _____

03 Gideon   _____   04 Deborah   _____

05 Samson   _____   06 Delilah   _____

07 Ruth   _____   08 Naomi   _____

09 Samuel   _____   10 Hannah   _____

(a) In order to fight the Midianites, I gathered many thousands of Israelite soldiers, but God permitted me only 300 men.

(b) My name means 'Yahweh is salvation.'

(c) I dedicated my son, Samuel to the LORD as long as he lived.

(d) I was the only female judge mentioned in the Bible.

(e) Samson fell in love with me, but I tricked him into telling the secret of his strength.

(f) I married Boaz, and our child, Obed, was an ancestor of David.

(g) I was living in Jericho and I hid two Israelite spies from the king.

(h) I had been forbidden by God to cut my hair since Mom conceived me.

(i) I lost my husband, Elimelech and two sons in Moab.

(j) When God called me, I answered, "Speak, for your servant is listening."

 ## C Grammar Test

01 다음 문장에서 밑줄 친 동사는 몇 형식으로 쓰인 것인지 적어보세요.

(a) God always <u>walks</u> with Joseph.

(b) God <u>set</u> a beautiful rainbow in the sky.

(c) That cake <u>tastes</u> good.

(d) Can you <u>give</u> me some water?

(e) Don't <u>call</u> me Naomi.

02 괄호 안의 동사를 적절한 시제로 바꿔보세요.

(a) I _____ (study) English every night.

(b) She _____ (listen to) music right now.

(c) I _____ (finish) my homework ten minutes ago.

(d) I _____ (play) the violin when you called me.

(e) Naomi _____ (live) happily with them after Ruth and Boaz got married.

(f) We _____ (go) to the movies tonight.

(g) I _____ (call) you tonight.

03 다음 질문에 적절한 대답을 써보세요.

(a) A: What do you do (for a living)?

    B: _____

(b) (At the beauty parlor)

    A: How much do you want to cut off?

    B: _____

Let's Enjoy Speed Game!

다음은 우리가 지금까지 공부했던 구약의 인물 카드입니다. 두 명씩 팀을 이루어 주어진 시간 안에 한 사람은 영어로 인물을 설명하고, 다른 한 사람은 그 설명을 듣고 인물의 이름을 맞혀보세요!

- 제한 시간은 임의로 결정하면 됩니다.

- 인물 카드는 절취선을 따라 하나씩 분리한 다음, 섞어서 사용하세요.

- 게임을 시작하기 전에 지금까지 공부한 내용을 다시 한 번 죽 훑어보며 인물의 특징을 다시금 정리해 보도록 합니다.

Adam

Eve

Cain

Abel

Noah

God

Isaac

Rebekah

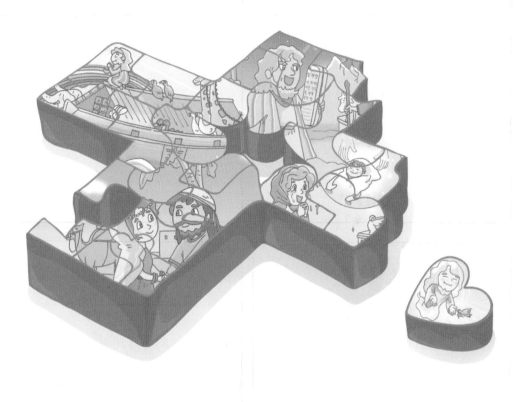

Jacob

Esau

Joseph

Reuben

Moses

Aaron

Joshua

Rahab

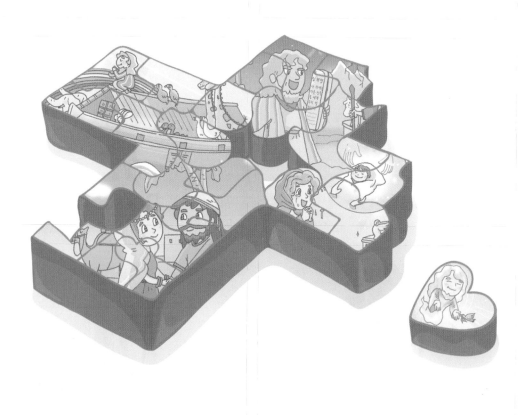

Gideon

Deborah

Samson

Delilah

Ruth

Naomi

Samuel

Hannah

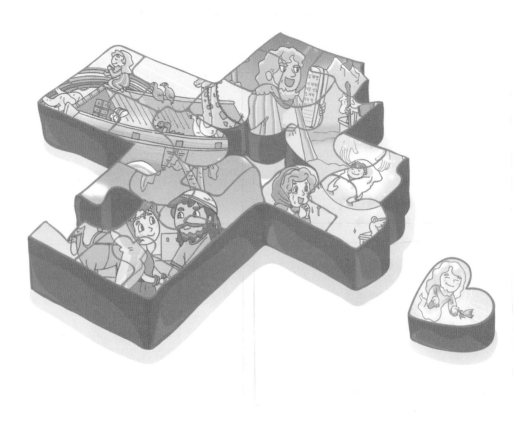

ANSWERS
for Grammar Points & Mini Test

02 • The First Murderer in the World

Grammar Points > Exercise 2

1 was jealous of **2** was good **3** are a famous couple **4** Cain looked angry

03 • The Righteous Man in the Corrupted World

Grammar Points > Exercise

1 rarely **2** always **3** rarely **4** rarely **5** always

▶ Minsu is a bad student.로 바꿔서도 문제를 풀어보세요.

04 • Father of Many Nations

Grammar Points > Exercise

1 타동사 **2** 자동사 **3** 타동사 **4** 자동사 **5** 자동사 **6** 타동사

Mini Test ①

A Dictation Test

01 create	**02** give in to	**03** get in trouble
04 shepherd	**05** wanderer	**06** jealousy
07 righteous	**08** ark	**09** destroy
10 prepare	**11** change	**12** slave

13 Noah always walked with God when everyone else became selfish and mean.

B Reading Comprehension Test

01 (c)　**02** (f)　**03** (b)　**04** (e)　**05** (a)　**06** (g)　**07** (h)　**08** (d)

C Grammar Test

01 (b)

02 (c)

03 (a) Minsu is <u>always</u> tired.

　　(b) Younghee <u>always</u> looks happy.

04 (a) 자동사　(b) 자동사　(c) 타동사

05 예 I was born in Seoul.

　　　▶ '~에서 태어났다'는 의미의 was born in을 활용하면 됩니다.

05 • The Son in Abraham's Old Age

Grammar Points > Exercise 1

1 명사　**2** 장소　**3** 형용사　**4** 장소　**5** 명사

Grammar Points > Exercise 2

1 We are at home

2 Jinhee is smart

3 Minsu and Jinhee are students

06 • Father of the Twelev Tribes of Israel

Grammar Points > Exercise

1 cell phone, give it to me

2 showed my student ID card to my teacher

3 pass me the salt

4 send us your resume by email

5 lend me your laptop

07 • The Dreamer and Dream Interpreter

Grammar Points > Exercise

1 made me clean/wash my hands

2 let, call you

3 Let me introduce myself.

08 • The Great Liberator of the Israelites

Grammar Points > Exercise

1 heard, calling

2 see, gather 또는 gathering

3 see, scolding

4 smell, burning

Mini Test ②

A Dictation Test

01 urge | **02** fury | **03** trick
04 blessing | **05** offer | **06** present (n.)
07 bow | **08** starvation | **09** descendant
10 plague | **11** prophet | **12** disobedience

13 I regret helping the people of Israel build a golden calf.

B Reading Comprehension Test

01 (d) **02** (e) **03** (g) **04** (b) **05** (c) **06** (h) **07** (a) **08** (f)

C Grammar Test

01 (c)

02 (a) I will lend some money to Minhee.

(b) I will give a birthday present to Mom.

03 (a) lent → lend (철자가 틀렸음) / to me it → it to me

(b) to change → change

(c) X (틀린 것 없음)

(d) to walk → walk 또는 walking

(e) X (틀린 것 없음)

04 예 I don't think so. Your English is good.

Activity ❷

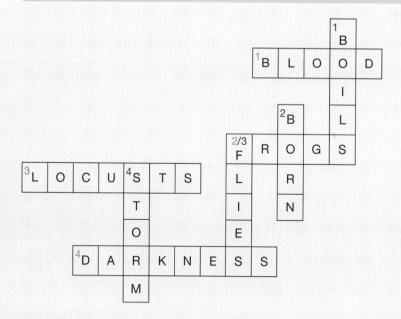

09 • Moses' Aide and Successor

Grammar Points > Exercise

1 5형식 **2** 4형식 **3** 1형식 **4** 2형식 **5** 3형식

10 • The Idol Breaker in the Age of Judges

Grammar Points > Exercise 1

1 study **2** is listening to **3** begin **4** drink **5** is beeping

Grammar Points > Exercise 2

1 is raining

2 often go out with my friends

3 are middle school students

11 • The Man with More-than-human Strength

Grammar Points > Exercise

1 were you doing / was running

2 did you do / called / slept

12 • The Faithful Daughter-in-law in Bethlehem

Grammar Points > Exercise

1 After I turned off the TV at 9:30, I went to bed at 10:00.

= I turned off the TV at 9:30 before I went to bed at 10:00.

2 After I took a shower at 7:00 a.m., I ate breakfast at 7:30 a.m.

= I took a shower at 7:00 a.m. before I ate breakfast at 7:30 a.m.

13 • The Attentive Listener to God Calling

Grammar Points > Exercise

1 are going to   **2** I'll call   **3** 두 개 다

4 will   **5** is going to

Mini Test 3

A Dictation Test

01 salvation   **02** warrior   **03** idol

04 kingship   **05** deliver   **06** entertain

07 pass away   **08** persuade   **09** relative

10 encourage

11 When God called him a fourth time, he answered, "Speak, for your servant is listening."

B Reading Comprehension Test

01 (b)   **02** (g)   **03** (a)   **04** (d)   **05** (h)   **06** (e)   **07** (f)   **08** (i)   **09** (j)   **10** (c)

C Grammar Test

01 (a) 1형식   (b) 3형식

    (c) 2형식   (d) 4형식

    (e) 5형식

02 (a) study

    (b) is listening to

    (c) finished

    (d) was playing

    (e) lived

    (f) are going 또는 are going to go

    (g) will call

03 (a) 예 I am a hairstylist. / I work at a hair salon.

      ▶ 〈I am + 직업명〉 또는 〈I work at + 장소〉를 활용하면 됩니다.

    (b) 예 I like this length.

176

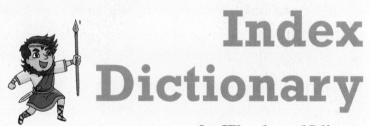

Index Dictionary
for Words and Idioms

advise: to give your opinion to someone about the best thing to do in a particular situation 조언하다

adultery: sex between someone who is married and someone who is not their wife or husband 간음

affirm: to state that something is true or that you agree with it. especially in public 인정하다, 승인하다

aide: someone whose job is to help another person in their work 보조자, 조력자

altar: a holy table used in religious ceremonies 제단

ancestor: someone who is related to you who lived a long time ago 선조

anoint: to put oil on a part of someone's body in a religious ceremony 기름을 붓다

apart from: except for someone or something ~와는 별개로

appealing: attractive and interesting 매혹적인

ark: a large ship 방주

as a result of: because of ~의 결과로

as well: in addition to something or someone else ~도 또한

attack: to attempt to harm a person. animal or place 공격하다

barley: a plant that produces grain used for making food. beer. and whiskey 보리

basket: a container for carrying or keeping things in 바구니

battle: a fight between two armies in a war 전투

bind: to tie someone's hands or feet together so they cannot move 꼼짝 못하게 묶다

birthright: a right. privilege. or possession to which a person is entitled by birth 장자상속권

bitter: making you feel very unhappy and upset 혹독한, 모진, 쓰라린

blessing: protection and help offered by God 축복, 은총

boast: to proudly tell other people about your abilities. achievements. or possessions 자랑하다

bow: to bend your body forwards from the waist. especially to show respect for someone 절하다

braid: a length of hair that has been separated into three parts and then woven together 땋은 머리

bury: to put something/somebody in the ground 파묻다, 매장하다

calf: a young cow 송아지

change: to make someone or something different 변경시키다

childless: not having any children 아이가 없는

come true: if something that you have hoped for or expected comes true. it really happens 실현되다

command: to tell someone officially to do something 명령하다

commander: one in an official position of command or control 지휘자

conceive: become pregnant 임신하다

concerned about: worried about something ~에 대해 걱정하는

condemn: to say publicly that you think someone or something is bad or wrong 비난하다

conquest: the process of taking control of land or people during a war 정복

coquettish: behaving in a way that is intended to attract men sexually 요염한, 교태 있는

court: a place where trials take place and legal cases are decided. especially in front of a judge and a jury 법정

covenant: a formal agreement or promise 언약

creation: the act of creating something 창조

create: to make something new or original that did not exist before 창조하다

curse: an offensive or very impolite word or phrase 저주

custom: something people do what is traditional or usual 관습

dedicate: to spend your time and effort doing something 헌신하다

defeat: to win against someone in a game. fight. or election 패배시키다

deliver: to free someone from an unpleasant situation 구해내다

deliverance: the process of being saved from danger or harm 해방

descendant: a relative of a person who lived in the past 후손

destroy: to damage something so severely that it no longer exists or can never return to its normal state 파괴하다

discover: to find out something that you did not know before 발견하다

disobedience: someone's behaviour when they do not obey orders or rules 불복종

displeased: annoyed or not satisfied 불쾌한

dispute: a serious disagreement. especially one between groups of people that lasts for a long time 분쟁

dominion: control or the right to rule over something 지배(권)

encourage: to suggest that someone does something that you believe would be good ～하라고 권하다, 격려하다

enemy: someone who is opposed to someone else and tries to do them harm 적

entertain: to give a performance that people enjoy 즐겁게 하다

ephod: an embroidered vestment believed to resemble an apron with shoulder straps. worn by priests 유대 제사장의 제의

excel: to do something extremely well 뛰어나다, 출중하다

famous: known about by many people in many places 유명한

figurative: using words not in their normal literal meaning but in a way that makes a description more interesting or impressive 비유적인

firstborn: someone's first child 첫째로 태어난, 맏이

flee: to escape from a dangerous situation or place very quickly 도망가다

flock: a group of birds, sheep or goats (새, 양, 염소 등의) 무리, 떼

flood: a large amount of water that covers an area that was dry before 홍수

forbid: to state that something is not allowed, according to a rule, law, or custom 금지하다

foreign: from another country, or in another country 외국의

fury: extreme, often uncontrolled anger 격노

gather: to bring things closer together 모으다

get in trouble: get in a situation for which you are likely to be blamed or punished 곤란한 지경에 빠지다

give in to: if you give in to something, you can no longer control the feeling of wanting it ~에 빠지다

glean: to pick up small amounts of the crops left in a field after they have been cut and collected by farmer 이삭을 줍다

guilty: ashamed and sorry because you have done something wrong 죄의식에 빠진, 죄책감을 느끼는

harvester: a machine or person that harvests crops 수확자

horn: one of the hard pointed parts that usually grow in a pair on the head of some animals 뿔

idol: a picture or statue that is worshipped as a god 우상

in return: as payment or in exchange for something 답례로, 보답으로

instead of: used for saying that one person, thing, or action replaces another ~대신에

instruction: a statement or explanation of something that must be done, often given by someone in authority 지시, 가르침

interfere: to deliberately get involved in a situation where you are not wanted or needed 간섭하다

interpret: to understand an action, situation, etc. in a particular way 해석하다

jealous of: feeling angry and unhappy because someone has something that you wish you had ~을 질투하는

kingship: the position of king 왕권

ladder: a piece of equipment used for climbing up to or down from high places. which has two bars that are connected by rungs (= short bars that you use as steps) 사다리

lap: the top half of your legs above your knees when you sit down 무릎

legal: allowed by the law 합법적인

lentil: a small round seed like a bean. dried and used for food 렌즈콩

lift: to move something to a higher position 들어 올리다

long for: to want something very much 갈망하다

mean: cruel or unkind 야비한

might (n.): great power or strength 힘

murderer: someone who commits murder 살인자

nation: a country that has its own land and government 국가

object: the person that people have a particular feeling about 대상

offer one's olive branch: to show that they want to stop arguing. The olive branch is often used as a sign meaning peace 화해를 청하다

offering: something that people give as a present to God 제물

offspring: someone's child or children 후손

pass away: to die 돌아가시다

permit: to allow someone to do something 허락하다

persuade: to make someone agree to do something by giving them reasons why they should 설득하다

pillar: a thick strong upright post that supports part of a building 기둥

plague: any serious disease that spreads quickly to a lot of people and usually ends in death 역병, 전염병

portion: a part of an amount or total 조각, 부분

position: someone's rank or status in an organization or in society 위치, 입장, 지위

pregnant: having a baby developing inside her body 임신한

prepare: to make something ready for use 준비하다

present: something that you give to someone. for example to celebrate a special occasion such as a birthday 선물

prevent: to stop someone from doing something 하지 못하게 막다

priest: someone whose job is to lead worship and perform other duties and ceremonies in some Christian churches 사제, 목사

prophet: a man sent by God to lead people and teach them their religious beliefs 예언자, 사제

prophetess: a woman who is a prophet 여사제

prostitute: someone. especially a woman. who is paid to have sex with people 창녀

protest: to say that you strongly disagree with or are angry about something because you think it is wrong or unfair 항의하다, 이의를 제기하다

prove: to provide evidence that shows that something is true 증명하다

put one's belief into action: to start using one's belief 믿음을 실행에 옮기다

question (v.): to have or express doubts about something 물어보다, 의문을 제기하다

ram: a male sheep 숫양

reed: a tall thin plant that grows near water 갈대

regard: attention or care that you give to someone or something 관심, 배려

reject: to not agree to an offer, proposal, or request 거절하다

rejoice: to feel very happy about something 기뻐하다, 좋아하다

relative: a member of your family, especially one who does not live with you 가족, 친척

release: to let someone leave a place where they have been kept 풀어주다

restore: to cause a particular situation to exist again, especially a positive one 회복시키다

rib: one of the long curved bones that are in your chest 갈비뼈

righteous: morally good or correct 의로운

Sabbath Day: a day for people of some religions to rest and pray 안식일

sacrifice: to give up something important or valuable so that you or other people can do or have something else 희생하다

salvation: the act of being saved by God from evil 구원

scarlet: bright red in color 주홍색

schemer: a person to make secret plans to achieve something, especially in a dishonest way 책략가

secret: a piece of information that is known by only a small number of people, and is deliberately not told to other people 비밀

seek (- sought - sought): to ask for something or try to get something 찾다, 추구하다

sensual: relating to or providing physical pleasure, especially sexual pleasure 관능적인

serpent: a snake, especially a large one 뱀

settle: to end an argument by making an agreement 해결하다

shepherd: a man whose job is to take care of sheep 양치기

sign: a piece of evidence that something is happening or that something exists 징조

sink: to disappear below the surface of the water 가라앉다

slave: someone who belongs by law to another person as their property and has to obey them and work for them 노예

sleeve: the part of a piece of clothing that covers your arm 소매

specific: limited to one particular thing 특정한

spy (v.): to work as a spy 염탐하다

staff: a long stick used for making walking easier 지팡이

stand: to be good or strong enough not to be badly affected or damaged by something 참다, 견디다

starvation: a situation in which a person or animal suffers or dies because they do not have enough to eat 굶주림, 아사

steal: to take something that belongs to someone else without permission 훔치다

stew: a dish made by cooking vegetables, and usually meat or fish, slowly in liquid 스튜

support: to provide money, food, shelter, or other things that someone needs in order to live 부양하다, 먹여 살리다

swear: to use words that are deliberately rude and offensive 욕하다

take care of: to do the necessary things for someone who needs help or protection 돌보다

take someone's place: to do something instead of someone else 대신하다

temple: a building used for worship in some religions 사원

temptation: a strong feeling of wanting to have or do something, especially something that is bad for you 유혹

throw: to use force to move someone 내치다

tribe: a large group of related families who live in the same area and share a common language, religion, and customs 부족

trick: to make someone believe something that is not true 속이다, 술수를 쓰다

twin: one of two children born at the same time to the same mother 쌍둥이

urge: to advise someone very strongly about what action or attitude they should take
(어떻게 하라고) 몰다

valley: a low area of land between mountains or hills. usually with a river flowing through it 계곡

wanderer: a person who travels from place to place. especially on foot. without a particular direction or purpose 방랑자

warning: an action or statement telling someone of a possible problem or danger 경고

warrior: a soldier 군인, 병사

wrestle: to fight by holding and pushing someone but without hitting with your fists 씨름하다

GOD IS SO GOOD

1. God is so good, God is so good,

God is so good, He's so good to me.

2. God loves me so, God loves me so,
   God loves me so, He's so good to me.
3. God answers prayer, God answers prayer,
   God answers prayer, He's so good to me.

MEMO

MEMO

MEMO

Ten Commandments

1. You shall have no other gods but Me.

2. Do not treat anything else as God.

3. You shall not use the name of the Lord to swear or curse.

4. You shall keep the Sabbath Day holy.

5. Honour your father and your mother.

6. You shall not commit murder.

7. You shall not commit adultery.

8. You shall not steal.

9. You shall not lie.

10. Do not long for other people's things.

(Exod. 20:1-17)